BLOOD
BROTHERS

BLOOD BROTHERS

To Battleground Smokeshell and Back

DEON LAMPRECHT

Delta Books

JOHANNESBURG & CAPE TOWN

First published in South Africa in 2024 by
DELTA BOOKS
A division of Jonathan Ball Publishers
A division of Media24 (Pty) Ltd
PO Box 33977
Jeppestown
2043

ISBN 978-1-92824-818-7
ebook ISBN 978-1-92824-819-4

*Every effort has been made to trace the copyright holders and
to obtain their permission for the use of copyright material.
The publishers apologise for any errors or omissions and would
be grateful to be notified of any corrections that should be
incorporated in future editions of this book.*

jonathanball.co.za
X.com/JonathanBallPub
facebook.com/JonathanBallPublishers

Cover design and typesetting by Johan Koortzen
Set in 11 pt on 15.5 pt Adobe Garamond Pro

CONTENT

Author's note   vii

PART 1 - THE ROAD TO SMOKESHELL

1. Demons of the bush   1
2. Braaivleis, rugby, sunny skies and ... army   6
3. The commandant and the lieutenant   15
4. The place of the camelthorn trees   28
5. Secret plans and premonitions of doom   42
6. Blood and fire in the bush   52
7. Heartbreak and heroism   79
8. A night on the killing field   101

PART 2 - BEYOND SMOKESHELL

9. HP and Phia   115
10. Marco and Pamela   136
11. Paul and Lynette   151
12. Other paths to healing: Gareth and Jan   171

PART 3 – BACK TO THE KILLING FIELD

13. The quest   193
14. Old friends reunited and healing in the bush   201
15. Reflections   223

An unplanned trilogy   236
About the Author   243

AUTHOR'S NOTE

Over time, the challenges, flaws, successes and lessons of the attack on the objective at Smokeshell have been chewed over by many a prominent historian, strategist and esteemed career officer.

This book is a humble effort to relate the story of Smokeshell to a wider audience and a much younger generation in the words of a few national servicemen – the survivors of Platoon 1, Bravo Company, which for all practical purposes ceased to exist on 10 June 1980.

And, equally important, the book attempts to tell the story of their lifelong journey of healing after that day of blood and fire in the Angolan bush.

THE ROAD TO SMOKESHELL

9J

1
DEMONS OF THE BUSH

After he shouts the command into the radio, the four Ratel combat vehicles roar up the bank of the dry riverbed and start ploughing through the bush in line abreast. Then all hell breaks loose …

Startled Swapo fighters, hundreds of them, scatter in all directions. Bullets clatter like hail against the armoured hulls of the Ratels. The gunners and riflemen of Paul Louw's platoon return fire with all they've got, but their main armament of 20 mm rapid-fire cannons jam and they're reduced to fighting with Browning machine guns, R1 assault rifles and hand grenades.

Amid the chaos of the battle, peering through the armoured glass of his turret sight blocks, Paul notices how old some of the enemy soldiers are compared to his own 19-year-old troopies. Uniformed and armed, yes, but with the tell-tale hue of many winters in their hair. Then one of the grey heads disappears in a spray of blood …

With a start he's jerked back into the present, shivering on his camping bed with his sleeping bag pulled over his head against the chilly Angolan night. He reassures himself yet again: 'This is 2022, the war has been over for a long time, you're safe. Everybody is safe.'

Suddenly a frightening new sound drowns out the crackling of the enemy's AK-47 assault rifles: PAAA-RAP-PAP-PAP-PAAARP! Like a giant motorcycle reverse-throttled by a demon rider. The young platoon leader needs nobody to tell him it is the manic scream of a Soviet ZU-23-2 anti-aircraft gun – and that it could tear through the metal hulls of his Ratels as if they were made of paper.

He struggles onto his back, with the sleeping bag wound tightly around his body. Above him the dense black of the Angolan night sky is shot through with the light of a trillion stars. Just like that night 42 years ago. He tries to count them – anything to sink back into the oblivion of sleep, to stop reliving that terrible battle.

But the demons that dwell in this godforsaken patch of bush continue to torment him.

Through his radio headset he hears the mix of adrenaline and fear in the voices of his section leaders. Some of his platoon vehicles that are packed with his boys are being hit, he realises with dread.

And then the interior of Paul's own Ratel becomes an inferno of smoke, flames and the loud popping sounds of munitions exploding in their storage bins.

He tries to grab his rifle from its rack but flames sear his arm and he bails out of the vehicle without it, shouting to his crew to take cover in an abandoned Swapo trench.

Voices in the night drag Paul back into the present. Anxiety takes hold: What if the local people decide to attack the invaders of the past, the small group of South African war veterans? What could I do? How would I protect them?

His torch beam leaps out to touch two young women, chatting

while they walk from one kraal to another. It's okay, he realises with a rush of relief. There's no problem. But he quickly switches off the torch because the last thing he wants to do, in this of all places, is to attract attention to himself. Once more he turns his gaze to the heavens and tries to lose his memories among the distant stars.

But the enveloping bush has no pity. As the hours drag by, Paul once again sees the faces of the dead and his nostrils fill with the terrible smell of charred flesh. And he relives that endless night trapped in a destroyed Ratel, surrounded by the enemy and praying to be rescued.

At first light, that false blue-grey dawn before the sun lifts its fiery head above the bush, his fellow veteran Andrew Whitaker comes stomping around the nose of the bakkie. He gives Paul a knowing look and comments wryly: 'The demons were busy with you last night …'

No explanation is needed, because Andrew knows. Those who have survived the horrors of war share a mutual understanding that goes beyond words. A nod from Paul confirms that his second night in the killing zone of Smokeshell was no picnic.

On 10 June 1980, during one of the toughest battles of the Border War, the sands of this place were drenched with the blood of his troops. Twelve died, another 17 were wounded. Of 44 young men, only 12 were left unharmed when the shooting stopped.

To locals, this piece of bush in southwestern Angola is known as Chifufua. But for the young South African national servicemen who fought here, many of them still in their teens, it will always remain 'Smokeshell' – the code name for one of the targets of Operation Sceptic. The attack on Smokeshell was the baptism of fire for a specialised new unit, 61 Mechanised Battalion

Group. The task of 61 Mech – as it would forever be called by its members – was to take the war to Swapo in its strongholds inside Angola. Smokeshell would also be the big test for 61 Mech's war horses – the Ratel infantry fighting vehicles designed for mobile warfare in the harsh African landscape.

From a military point of view, Smokeshell was successful. A vast Swapo command complex was destroyed, about 370 enemy soldiers killed and tonnes of vehicles and munitions hauled back across the border. But hard lessons were learned by the South Africans and a high price in blood was paid.

For decades the survivors bore the trauma of that day and relived it in a thousand nightmares. For the smell of diesel, smoke and fresh blood never leaves you.

As the years passed, the battlefield was reclaimed by the ever-patient bush. The old Swapo trenches were filled with wind-blown sand and leaves. There were no real landmarks to start with. The location was soon forgotten.

But one man was determined to find it and bring the young men he once led back to the place where they had fought so long ago. To pay tribute to their fallen comrades and lay their demons to rest. That man, retired General Johann Dippenaar, started searching obsessively for the site of Smokeshell – and eventually found it.

Four decades after that hellish battle, Dippenaar returned with seven other Smokeshell veterans he had led as a commandant. Men like Paul, who was only too relieved that daybreak made his demons retreat. And the legendary Hennie 'HP' Ferreira, who was the driver of Paul's Ratel. During the battle a round from a 14,5 mm machine gun tore away most of HP's coccyx, intestine and stomach. Since that day, he's had more than a hundred surgical procedures.

Under the uncaring eye of the morning sun, the small group starts walking along the dirt path to a tree among the old trenches. Camping chairs are set out under its branches and a banner covers a simple memorial.

Emotion chokes the air like the lingering plume of dust raised by a convoy of Ratels. For the blood brothers of Smokeshell, it's been a long and arduous journey back to the killing field.

2

BRAAIVLEIS, RUGBY, SUNNY SKIES AND ... ARMY

In 1979–1980, a bright future beckoned for the generation of South African boys fresh from the school classrooms of white suburbia. They were young and healthy, and life held many opportunities.

Back then, you could buy a shiny new Datsun 120Y for R40 000 and fill her up at the pump for 47 cents a litre. Treating your girl to a 'prawn special' would set you back R10 a head, and a bottle of cheap white wine another ten bucks. Movie after dinner? The second *Star Wars* film, *The Empire Strikes Back*, blazed over screens across the globe. Locally, the romantic student comedy *Kiepie en Kandas* made it big, and for action seekers there was the Border War movie *Grensbasis 13*.

For mood music during a sweaty smooching session outside your sweetheart's parental home, you might have slipped the latest Pink Floyd album into your car's tape deck. When you pressed your face into your shirt the next morning, the heady smell of her Charlie perfume still clung to it.

Because of the international sports boycott against the South African government's policy of apartheid, the rugby-mad public hungered for top-level contests. Small wonder, then, that the pending arrival of the British and Irish Lions caused a froth of excitement. Lanky Morné du Plessis captained the Springboks and Naas Botha's sniping boot was expected to vanquish the invaders on the field.

At the same time, Gerrie 'Seer Handjies' Coetzee was giving the punching bag hell as he prepared for his second assault on the world heavyweight boxing title. Squaring up to him in the ring at Sun City would be American fighter Mike Weaver.

Domestically, the political pot was approaching boiling point, but most whites were blissfully unaware of the true nature and extent of the freedom struggle. There was a vague awareness of 'trouble in the townships' but protective suburban bubbles remained intact.

And few people 'back home' knew how heated the Border War in the north of South West Africa (today Namibia) really was. The National Party government and the South African Defence Force (SADF) controlled the flow of information and news about the war. Security legislation was in place to silence the media. Only journalists with special accreditation (granted after background checks to ensure you were not a subversive) could report on military affairs – and then under strict conditions. The letters from the troops in the operational area to their loved ones back home were censored and they, too, lived under the cloud of the Official Secrets Act.

Over all this presided Prime Minister PW Botha. On television, in parliament and at public events he warned with a dour face and wagging finger of the 'total onslaught' of communism against South Africa, the 'last bastion' of freedom in southern Africa. There was no real public counter to this narrative because there were no independent television channels, no foreign news channels, no internet and no social media.

Public fear of the threat posed by Soviet-backed liberation movements was fuelled by the bloody war in neighbouring Rhodesia (today Zimbabwe), which was fast approaching its inevitable end. In Afrikaans movies such as *Kaptein Caprivi* and *Aanslag op Kariba* the 'terrorists' always met a bad end. And popular picture-book heroes such as Kaptein Duiwel and Grensvegter dispatched the enemy with cheesy speech bubbles.

Against this background, compulsory military service was just a normal part of life for white South African boys. The Cadet Corps was an integral part of the school system. Once a week, boys went to school in cadet uniforms – basically a short-trousered version of the standard military combat uniform known as 'browns'. You knew how to wear your beret with attitude, with the silver Springbok emblem just so above your left eye. Male teachers stood in front of the blackboard in their uniforms with officers' insignia on their shoulders.

For an hour of your school day, you drilled on the rugby field, played in the marching band or plinked targets on the school shooting range with .22 rifles. During school cadet camps you learned how to camouflage and ambush each other at night. It was common to see older brothers on weekend pass showing off in their 'step outs' (formal uniforms). Schoolgirls were encouraged to write to troopies to boost their morale, and radio programmes played sentimental requests for 'our boys on the Border'.

This, in a nutshell, was the South Africa of the Smokeshell generation. A diverse group of boys of 18 or 19 years old. For some of them, the flames of patriotism and duty burned brightly; for others, it was the first great adventure of their young lives. Still others merely wanted to get the rite of passage known as *diensplig* (national service) behind them so they could get on with their lives. The alternative for those with political or moral objections was discouraging at best: a prison sentence or exile. The End Conscription Campaign did not exist at the time. In any case, the thought of defying the law of the land would not have crossed many minds. When young men got those brown envelopes with their call-up instructions, the vast majority simply obeyed: they were taught to see it as their duty and they went with the blessing of their parents, teachers and churches.

Among those who obeyed the call was Hennie 'HP' Ferreira, a farm kid from Theunissen, and later Welkom, in the Free State.

HP cared little for his schoolbooks, but he could do just about anything with his hands and he was a born entrepreneur. In his boarding-school room he dispensed haircuts for pocket money or he would sneak out to buy packets of steaming, vinegary 'slap' chips from the Greek's corner café for 15 cents each and resell them for double the price. The matric boys who crammed for exams in the study hall at night were only too happy to pay up. Most of all, HP loved to run. Barefooted on the farm or on the athletics track, HP could run like a hare all day.

With little interest in academic prowess, he decided to leave school in Standard 8 (Grade 10 today), rather than hang in there for another two years to obtain a 'practical matric' certificate. This meant he would have to report for military service straight away. But, even so, he would still have a two-year head start in life over his classmates, he reasoned.

On the other side of the coin were guys like Gareth Rutherford, from Kalk Bay, who has the soul of a philosopher and loves to

Marco Caforio as young national serviceman.

pour out his emotions, thoughts and observations on paper. It helps him to make sense of what has happened to him on any given day.

And Paul Louw from Bloemfontein, who excelled on the rugby field and in the school choir. His greatest ambition was to be a man like the father he lost at too young an age: a man who was both a scholar and a commanding officer in the Citizen Force, the military reserve force of the time.

Or Marco Caforio, who grew up in the 'exotic' neighbourhood of Orange Grove in Johannesburg. As the son of an Italian immigrant, he was not legally obliged to do national service, but his father, the proud owner of a pizza restaurant, felt the family had to pay their dues to the country that had adopted them.

Jan Hoevers, from Ermelo, suffered from dyslexia, a learning disorder little understood by educators back then. He left school at the earliest opportunity and joined South African Railways as an assistant train driver. As this was considered a key job, he was exempted from military service.

Even on the rails his dyslexia held him back, and Jan made a crucial decision: to succeed in life, he had to be his own boss. This meant he would have to do his national service after all, because he had not worked on the trains long enough to be exempted for life. Jan always trusted his instincts, which is why, when the bulky envelope from the Department of Defence arrived, he did not ask his boss to sign the usual deferment application.

In the envelope was a list of the odd things you had to buy before reporting for duty and the chance to be turned into a soldier: an electric clothes iron; a bath plug; a tin of floor polish; Brasso to shine buttons, buckles and badges; shoe polish of course (Kiwi dark brown, nothing else would do); a box of washing powder; clothes pegs; a matching set of three brass padlocks; and – oddest of all – a metre of chain. (This, you would learn, was to chain your laundry to the washing line to prevent it from being stolen.)

Then dawned the day of your departure by troop train from your home town. Mothers tried to hide their tears, while fathers stoutly assured their sons that the army would make them into men. As the train pulled away, long-haired boys hung in clusters from carriage windows and waved until they disappeared from sight.

Each year, the rail system ferried tens of thousands of recruits to bases all over the country, where their heads were shorn by crusty, chain-smoking barbers. But for HP, Gareth, Marco and Jan the destination was Bloemfontein, where the bawling, cursing corporals of 1 South African Infantry Battalion (1 SAI) awaited the latest batch of *rowe* (Afrikaans for scabs, as raw recruits were called).

Some of the lads on the train to Bloemfontein were quiet and introspective; others joked around in a display of bravado. But all were ignorant of developments thousands of kilometres away in South West Africa, where the war was spreading like a veld fire.

All too soon, it would have a devastating impact on their young lives.

The first shots of the Border War proper were fired in 1966, when guerrillas of the South West African People's Organisation (Swapo) first clashed with units of the South African Police (SAP) and the SADF in the far north of the territory.

South Africa had governed South West Africa as a de facto fifth province since 1915, after liberating it from German colonial forces during World War I. In the mid-1960s, Swapo, which had been founded in 1960, decided to turn to armed conflict to further its liberation struggle. The conflict escalated dramatically in 1975, when Portugal ended its colonial reign in neighbouring Angola and civil war broke out among the various Angolan factions. South Africa invaded Angola clandestinely in 1975 to prevent the Soviet-backed Popular Movement for the Liberation of Angola (MPLA) from coming to power but failed in that mission. Once in power, the MPLA offered support to Swapo and allowed the group to establish bases in Angola.

By 1978–1979, Swapo incursions into South West Africa were increasing at an alarming rate. From their bases in Angola, where they were out of reach of South African security forces, guerrilla fighters of PLAN (People's Liberation Army of Namibia, the armed wing of Swapo) crossed the long border, using the bush as cover and a source of food and water. They attacked rural communities and farms, planted landmines, destroyed infrastructure such as electricity pylons, distributed propaganda leaflets and recruited more fighters and informants.

When the security forces started to pursue them, using trackers and Casspir mine-protected vehicles, the Swapo fighters slipped back over the border. Some simply buried their uniforms and weapons and disappeared into local communities until it was safe to strike again. For when they took up arms, they knew there were only two possible outcomes for their armed struggle: either they would achieve their dream of independence or die fighting. Going home after two years, like the boys from the farms and towns of South Africa, was never an option.

With civilian deaths in the farm communities and Ovambo trust area in the far north of South West Africa on the rise, and an escalation in firefights between the security forces and the insurgents, the generals in Pretoria decided to take the fight to the enemy. To act rather than react.

The change in strategy called for a new iron fist that could destroy Swapo in its bases in Angola. A highly mobile, cross-border fighting force that could range far afield and strike with devastating speed and firepower before withdrawing. The senior leadership of this new unit would consist of a small core of Permanent Force (regular) officers, but about 90 per cent – the gunners, drivers, riflemen, signallers, medics and tiffies (mechanics) – would be young national servicemen, as would the lieutenants and corporals who would lead them at platoon and section level.

By the time the boys of the Smokeshell generation reported for basic training in Bloemfontein in January 1979, the unit that would be immortalised as 61 Mechanised Battalion Group was already starting to take shape at Omuthiya, just north of the world-famous Etosha Game Reserve (today Etosha National Park). In this new base under the camelthorn trees, 61 Mech would be honed for their baptism of fire in Angola.

3

THE COMMANDANT AND THE LIEUTENANT

By 1979, the SADF had started to invest in mechanised warfare in a big way. It demanded new thinking, new weapon systems and new battle tactics. Much of this was to be tested and refined on the battlefield in real time amid bullets and bombs. The choreographer of this deadly dance by combined artillery, armour and mechanised infantry was the battle group commander – a senior Permanent Force officer. However, the junior leaders at the front of the fight were national servicemen with the temporary ranks of second lieutenant and corporal. The burden of responsibility on their young shoulders was enormous – as the battle for Smokeshell would clearly show.

As a young boy, the founder and commander of South Africa's first mechanised infantry fighting force, Johann Dippenaar, actually wanted to be a dominee (minister).

When Voortrekker Hoër in Bethlehem broke up for the December holidays, he closed the door of his hostel room in a state of great excitement and departed for the family farm near Petrus Steyn in the Free State. 'It was the highlight of my year ... to be able to spend my days in the veld, hunting birds with the pellet gun among the bluegum trees,' he recalls. 'My dad also had a farm in Botswana and, as I grew older, we would go hunting there. My love for the outdoors and rifles just grew and grew.'

At school he was a leader in the Cadet Corps, something he thoroughly enjoyed. You'd think that this – combined with his love for weapons, hunting and the outdoors – would have made a military career his first choice. But no, he had other ideas.

'Since my childhood, the church was a part of my life. And as a young lad I had this idea that I wanted to become a dominee,' Dippenaar told me at his home in Pretoria.

In his matric year he was dismayed to learn that Latin was a required subject: 'Man, that took the wind out of my sails. I could not even spell Latin, never mind master it. So, right there, I dropped the idea of studying theology.'

Shortly after that, he won the 'lottery', also known as the military drafting system, which at the time randomly selected some young men, but not all, to undergo military training. 'So I had no choice, I had to go. Back then, grounds for exemption barely existed.'

He duly reported to the Army Gymnasium in Heidelberg in 1962 and was assigned to the armoured group of 'about 120 strong'. After three months of basic training he was selected for the leadership course in Potchefstroom.

He did well but was told he was too young to become an officer. Instead he was rewarded with the stripes of a corporal and as such he completed his draft period. Back on civvy street, Dippenaar was still unsure of his future path. With theology no longer an option, he felt drawn to a career in accounting: 'I went to the University of Pretoria to check it out, to see what it would entail.'

But he felt overwhelmed by life in a big city. 'From a Free State farm to Pretoria ... It seemed like a Sodom and Gomorrah to me. I felt lost. I wanted to feel anchored in an environment that was familiar to me.'

What was familiar was the military life and routine he had just left. So he went back and told the authorities that Corporal Dippenaar was reporting for a career in the army. He was hopeful that joining the army would help him make the adjustment from farm life to the madhouse that was life in the big city.

And thus he started his long and distinguished career in the Armoured Corps as an instructor 'teaching recruits how to march and shoot' at Voortrekkerhoogte, the vast military complex outside Pretoria. He loved it: 'I'm somebody who adapts quickly. When given a task, I orientate myself and then I perform it successfully.'

Unbeknown to him, this adaptability would one day benefit him in the fast-moving, fluid arena of mechanised warfare.

From Voortrekkerhoogte, he was transferred to the armoured unit at Walvis Bay, the South African enclave wedged between the Atlantic Ocean and the dunes of the Namib Desert. There, Corporal Dippenaar learned how the elements could wear down the machinery of war: 'Not just the desert sand but also the salty moisture from the sea. The base was 20 km inland, but when those fog banks rolled in everything was wet for hours until the sun broke through. And then everything dried in a flash.'

The only way to combat the resulting crust of salt and rust on metal components was constant maintenance. This experience would serve him well in the conditions he would one day face in southern Angola. In that harsh environment he also learned the value of comradeship between men who have been shipped off to some remote spot and have to work together to get the job done, no matter what.

17

Career soldiers are rolling stones and one day he was told to pack his bags and return to Pretoria. There, he was informed that he was no longer too young to be a lieutenant, and off he went again – this time to Oudtshoorn for the gruelling officer's course. He describes it as 'the type of training that gives you a grounding of discipline and teaches you to work together and plan'.

With shiny new pips on his shoulders, Dippenaar was transferred to 1 Special Service Battalion (1 SSB) in Bloemfontein, where he started to learn how armour, infantry and artillery work together as a fighting force on the battlefield – essential learning for the pioneering work he would later do.

From Bloemfontein he was transferred to Zeerust (in present-day North West province). There, he witnessed how fatigued drivers got after spending long hours behind the wheel of an armoured car. Years later, in the Angolan bush, he would always ensure that drivers had regular breaks. Another practical lesson concerned map-reading and navigation: 'Yes, there were maps of the areas we had to travel through but they lacked detail. You had to depend on the junior leaders. If you tasked one of them to travel to point X along a specific route and they missed it, the bigger plan went to pot.'

From Zeerust, Dippenaar went on to the Army College in Pretoria for courses that would bring more knowledge, skills and promotions. And then, finally, he got his first taste of the real thing: 'In 1977, I was transferred to the former Rhodesia, a totally new and different experience. My wife and our three very young kids went with me. Lock, stock and barrel as they say.'

It would be their home for more than a year. Dippenaar continued his leadership training with the Rhodesian army, then in the thick of its own counterinsurgency war: 'Rhodesia was a huge learning curve – it was a foreign nation and a military which had a way of doing things that I was not familiar with. I joined them on operations and observed how they went about it. They made sure they had good visual observation of the enemy from the air while directing the ground assault. That was one of the outstanding lessons I learned over there.'

His stay in Rhodesia came to an abrupt end because of a pending visit by US Secretary of State Henry Kissinger. The latter was not supposed to see any signs of military collaboration between the two white-ruled southern African countries: 'It came as quite a shock when I heard that I had to leave the country within 24 hours. I was simply told: "Pack your stuff, a truck will collect everything tomorrow and then you leave." And that's how it happened; within two days my wife and kids and I were out of there.'

Back in South Africa, they were assigned a military house at Voortrekkerhoogte: 'It was unfurnished and, at first, we had to make do with donations from our families. We lived there for the next few years while I worked at Army Headquarters in Pretoria.'

He disliked his new desk job, which was all about the paper war needed to organise units. But everything changed the day he was told to vacate his office. He was to report to none other than the Chief of the Army, General Constand Viljoen, to serve as his personal staff officer.

Unbeknown to Dippenaar, his diverse career paths were about to converge: 'In hindsight this was one of the most important moments in my career as a soldier. Working so close to General Viljoen, I got the complete picture of how the army and its components worked as a whole. The general was the ultimate professional soldier. He did not put up with nonsense, but you could always go to him for advice or help. He listened objectively to find solutions and acted with sound judgement.'

It was Viljoen who dispatched Dippenaar to Angola in May 1978. The occasion was Operation Reindeer, a major offensive against Swapo command and logistical centres. The world tends to link Operation Reindeer solely with the airborne assault on Cassinga by paratroopers under the command of the legendary Colonel Jan Breytenbach. But there was a second target: the Swapo base complex at Chetequera, about 40 km inside Angola. This assault was the first by an SADF mechanised infantry force.

This fledgling force, led by Commandant Frank Bestbier, was dubbed Combat Group Juliet and Dippenaar was sent along as an observer. The assault on Chetequera was a success story for the new Ratel infantry fighting vehicle, and for Dippenaar it offered a glimpse of his very near future. Just a few months later, on yet another routine tour of SADF bases, Viljoen turned to Dippenaar and quietly dropped a clanger.

'I'll never forget that moment. We were flying on the chopper from a unit in East London to the next one when Viljoen said to me: "How would you like to go command a mechanised force in South West Africa?"'

For a moment Dippenaar was at a loss for words: 'I had no idea what he was talking about. All I heard were the words "mechanised" and "the Border". But that was enough to switch me on and I replied: "I'll take it, can't wait, when do I leave?"'

Be patient, Viljoen replied, it's not time yet.

But that same December, Dippenaar had to pack up his life yet again. By January 1979 – when the raw recruits of the Smokeshell generation were getting off the train in Bloemfontein with the shouts and curses of corporals assaulting their ears – Dippenaar was already in South West Africa as the first commander of 61 Mech.

20

Paul Louw was only two years old when his father, Johan, died.

As the youngest of three children in the family home in Bloemfontein, he doted on stories about the man he never knew. And, as far back as Paul can remember, he wanted to be like his dad. A man who was a career academic on the one hand and a military commander on the other. Or, as Paul puts it: 'A man with a degree who is also a commandant in the army.'

That dream would become one of the driving forces of his life.

'My dad was an only child and a very bright guy, from all I've heard. He was raised on the family farm in Reitz in the Free State, but his parents decided he had the potential to go to a top school. So they moved from the farm to a smallholding just east of Bloemfontein.'

They enrolled their son at the prestigious Grey College, where by all accounts he lived up to expectations. 'He was head boy of Grey in, I think, 1944. He did well in his studies, enjoyed the Cadet Corps and later became a Springbok rifle shot.'

He was studying geology at the University of the Orange Free State when he met his future wife, Jo, who was studying medicine. His dad loved the veld and geology, Paul recalls, but after completing his studies he joined the military, where he rubbed shoulders with future stars like Constand Viljoen.

As a career officer, he served in 1 SSB, the armoured unit in Bloemfontein where Dippenaar would also serve. And when he decided to return to civilian life, he did not close his military chapter. To cut a long story short, the man Paul wanted so much to emulate became both a lecturer in geology and a commandant of Regiment President Steyn, a Citizen Force unit based in Bloemfontein.

'He would have been very proud to know that President Steyn

was the first South African tank regiment to enter into battle since the Second World War.' (The regiment's Olifant tanks fought in some of the actions around Cuito Cuanavale near the end of the Border War.)

Paul was so determined to follow in his dad's big boots that he bought a Grey College tracksuit with his pocket money while he was still in his final year at Willem Postma Primary School. But things didn't work out that way because Jo had left her job as a medical researcher to qualify as a teacher. She got a teaching post at the rival Sentraal High School in Bloemfontein, so that was where Paul went.

'I'm mad about sport so I did not spend too much time with the books,' he confesses. 'I played rugby, hockey and cricket.' But the big, athletic teenager also played a leading role in the school choir.

His first real experience of death was near the end of his school career. Paul and his close friend Wessel were looking forward to reporting to 3 South African Infantry Battalion (3 SAI) together for their national service stint. But during their final school holiday, while helping his father on their sheep farm near Niekerkshoop, Wessel unexpectedly collapsed and died.

The headmaster of Sentraal took Paul and other schoolboys to Niekerkshoop, where they carried Wessel's coffin: 'Looking back at those years you realise what a protected childhood we had. Before that day I was kept away from funerals and that kind of thing. Then suddenly you're carrying a close friend of the last five years or so to his grave … Today I know that it helped prepare me for the army.'

Specifically, for the loss of so many troops that was to follow.

His love for sport proved a blessing during the grind of basic training at 3 SAI: 'I was so fit that the corporals couldn't break me during those endless opfoks [punishment exercises]. I mostly just laughed at them.'

After basics, he was accepted for junior leadership training at the Infantry School in Oudtshoorn. Once again, his athleticism proved its value: 'Our platoon leader told me: "Louw, I can't do anything to you. I can't fuck you up because you're too fit. You're laughing at me, but at least you're also making the platoon laugh." So I was always encouraging the other guys to hang in there when the going got tough.'

One of the infamous trials of physical and mental endurance for Infantry School students was the gruelling stage called *vasbyt* (hang in there): 'During *vasbyt* they pushed you as hard as they could. In the Swartberge we shivered through the nights in snow eight inches deep. I walked until my boots and feet were done. On the third day I went to our platoon commander and said: "I can carry on but not with my boots and feet in this condition, something must be done about them."

He was convinced they would kick him off the course there and then, but fate works in mysterious ways. For one of the other course members had died and as a result their *vasbyt* was suspended.

Back then, Paul had no idea that he and a handful of others would embark on a desperate *vasbyt* through the enemy-infested Angolan bush little more than a year later.

As he neared the end of the junior leader's course, Paul had no idea where he wanted to go next. Once again fate intervened, this time in the guise of a battle demonstration for foreign observers at Oudtshoorn. He saw Ratels in action for the first time: 'And I thought to myself: "Okay, I know the Ratels are based at 1 SAI in Bloem." So then I applied for the mechanised infantry.'

When he was marched in for the selection interview he was,

thanks to his rugby prowess, confronted by a familiar figure: Colonel Frank Bestbier. 'And he said to me: "Listen here, I think you just want to go to Bloemfontein to be close to your mom." So I said that will be a bonus, but I really want to do mech.'

Whether Bestbier believed him or not, Paul was soon on his way back to Bloem and 1 SAI, the training unit that would provide the infantry soldiers for Dippenaar's new South West Africa-based iron fist.

In Bloemfontein, the man charged with producing a new breed of infantry officer for the battlefield was the legendary (then major) Ep van Lill. With the physique of a wrestler and a black moustache of note, he would play a key role in the development of mechanised warfare tactics.

Van Lill had been one of the infantry commanders under Bestbier during Operation Reindeer. There, he realised that the way infantry fought on the ground was outdated. New tactics were needed to engage and destroy enemy soldiers in their trenches and bunkers. Back at 1 SAI, he built an assault course where recruits could be trained in tactics loosely based on the dark art of house clearing, as used in urban warfare. It was close-up, dirty stuff. He effectively became the architect of *loopgraafopruiming*, or trench clearing.

Van Lill would later become a commander of 61 Mech and, as such, lead the battle group during Operation Askari in Angola (1984). But that was still in the future when Paul and his fellow trainees reported to him in Bloemfontein.

'Oom Ep always impressed you as this utterly fearsome and formidable character,' Paul recalls. 'He was a qualified paratrooper and always wore his jumping boots. When you messed up during training he would kick your shins with those boots.'

A well-prepared Swapo bunker at Smokeshell.

The course was tough. Lots of physically demanding training, the never-ending routine of spit-and-polish and inspections, and plenty of theoretical coursework to do after the daily grind: 'I just decided they are not going to get me down. We burned the midnight oil to master the theory. It was then that I learned what it takes to study at night, for I never did so at school. But we studied hard, worked together, wrote our tests and passed. And we enjoyed the work.'

Ep van Lill taught his students one valuable lesson: it's good to do things according to the book, 'but when the shooting starts the book becomes obsolete, everything changes. Then you have to go from plan A to plans B or C ... You always have to have a plan.'

This was part of their practical training, 'but we never went beyond plan C'. Paul remembers wryly. 'After that there was nothing.'

Another truth of war was that 'softening up' the target with aerial and artillery bombardments was never enough. The only way to take and hold the objective was to send the infantry into the enemy trenches on foot to finish the job. 'Oom Ep' drilled his students in trench clearing until they were on the point of collapse.

Move along the trench in single file, when you reach the dark mouth of a bunker flatten yourself against the trench wall and toss in a grenade. WHOOMP! Your buddy comes past you from behind and fires a quick double tap inside before you move in to check for any surviving threat. Onwards and repeat, always covering your buddy's back. Over and over, first dry runs and then using live ammo. Until this deadly choreographed dance was second nature, because one day your life would depend on it.

When things went wrong on the training field, the consequences could be as fatal as on the battlefield, as Paul learned during one trench assault.

'They tossed the grenade into the bunker and the second guy came charging round but suddenly realised there had been no detonation yet … He threw himself backwards but as he did so it went off and shrapnel pierced his heart.'

Everybody was shocked but training soon continued: 'That's the gruesome nature of situations like that. You can't ignore or avoid it; you have to go back and do the job better next time.'

Finally the course ended and Paul, like everybody else who made the grade to lieutenant, had to indicate how he wanted to be deployed for the remainder of his national service.

'I wrote that I wanted to remain in Bloemfontein as an instructor. Because I wanted to keep on playing rugby: we had a great 1 SAI team going. Then Oom Ep summoned us one by one.'

Van Lill wasted no words. 'I don't even want to talk to you. You're going up north to the Border and that's that. I've already assigned you as a platoon commander, end of discussion.'

Thus was Second Lieutenant Paul Louw's course set for the hell of Smokeshell.

4

THE PLACE OF THE CAMELTHORN TREES

One day in January 1979, Commandant Dippenaar embarked on his great adventure. The Armoured Corps officer herded his family into the gaping belly of a Flossie, as the big C-130 Hercules transport planes were affectionately known. Destination: Oshakati, 2 000 km northwest of their Pretoria departure point. Mission: to build 61 Mech from the ground up.

'It was a totally different kind of experience. Very few units were ever established in that manner,' Dippenaar relates in his usual calm and understated way. 'At Oshakati we were assigned a house. But then I asked, "Where's the unit?" And I was told, no, there's just a few vehicles, but they're parked back in Grootfontein.'

Grootfontein was the gateway to the operational area. Through it flowed fresh troops and war materiel from 'the States' (South Africa) to the far north. And the *oumanne* (troops who had completed their operational stints) and casualties flowed back south and home.

Oshakati was 300 km north of Grootfontein, and thus Dippenaar had to travel back south to where his promised vehicles awaited. Upon arrival he realised they were the Ratels he had seen in action during Operation Reindeer the previous year. They were

Johann Dippenaar as a commandant.

pretty battered and less than one-tenth of the number of vehicles he would need.

But his troops, one company of seasoned national servicemen from 1 SAI, were not at Grootfontein. Instead, they were lolling around in tents further north at Oshivelo, the checkpoint where you crossed the 'red line' into the vast operational area.

Now Dippenaar had reason to be grateful for the paper shuffling he so disliked back at Army Headquarters in Pretoria: 'You just had to keep asking for the stuff you wanted and then fix it up with whatever was needed, like the appropriate radios and weapons systems. And then test it to make sure it was all serviceable and operationally ready.

'So, January '79 was a fairly difficult time, because I had a unit to build with only two guys to help me. But, in reality, they were not qualified for the job; they could at best lend a hand here and there. And all the equipment for these vehicles had to be acquired. And as it started to arrive piecemeal, so did the soldiers.'

His next big decision was where to base the unit that was slowly starting to take shape, 'as the whole of Ovamboland lay open before me'.

Dippenaar wanted a central location for his base so that he could move his force in any direction as the situation demanded. So he got behind the wheel of a 'gharrie', as Land Rovers were sometimes known in the army, and started to explore the area. Just above the northeastern corner of the Etosha Game Reserve, he found the right place. Omuthiya, local people called it, which means 'camelthorn trees'.

He had an instant liking for this place, where so many of the hardy trees of the region were clumped together: 'You're in nature. And there's water, very brackish, but water nonetheless. Of equal importance was that Omuthiya was tucked away from prying eyes.'

The next thing was to start visualising the base that was to take shape in the virgin bush: 'I don't think anybody had any idea what it was supposed to look like. So I just started pacing off big squares and saying one company's tent lines will be here, another company's over there, and so on.'

Dippenaar had plenty of pacing to do under those camelthorn trees, for at that stage the unit would comprise a mechanised infantry company, an armoured squadron, an artillery battery, sappers (engineering corps) and signallers. And of course those miracle workers called 'tiffies' – the mechanics in uniform who would fix and maintain anything, from vehicles to weapons systems, on the base or in the field.

Apart from men and weapons, Omuthiya would house a lot of vehicles – from the Ratel combat vehicles to the logistical trucks carrying diesel, water, rations, ammunition, spare parts and everything else needed to keep a mechanised force moving and fighting. Dippenaar's headquarters alone would be borne along by four Ratels.

'As the troops started arriving, we assigned them areas where they had to clear the bush, pitch their tents and dig trenches for protection … So it was a hectically busy time at Omuthiya.'

Much of the initial construction – rows of cement slabs for troop tents, a mess big enough to seat and feed a thousand men, ablution blocks, storerooms, the great hangars for lines of Ratels, the vehicle workshop area – was done by the infantry *oumanne* Dippenaar found at Oshivelo. The were ably assisted and directed by a troop of engineers.

But, despite all the work going on, it was still a wild place. The nearby Etosha Game Reserve was not wholly fenced yet and sometimes elephants would stride through the tent lines like great, grey ghosts in the moonlight.

The troops adopted any animal, from bush babies to a zebra foal and a python, as pets and found inventive ways to spirit them away when the brass wanted to 'liberate' the animals. For entertainment, scorpion and spider fights were organised.

'They were just like troops everywhere, always up to something,' Dippenaar recalls fondly. 'If things are too quiet in camp you know there's mischief afoot.'

But work and play at Omuthiya ground to a sudden halt in May 1979, when a big group of Swapo fighters crossed over from Angola and swiftly infiltrated the rural areas south of the border.

'One moment I was busy sorting out Ratel and Eland armoured

cars for the unit, the next I was told to drop everything and redeploy to Tsumeb … The terrs were in and members of the Roodt and Friederich families were murdered on their farms.'[1]

It was the start of the counterinsurgency operation Awake, later renamed Operation Carrot. The war was no longer hundreds of kilometres away in Angola, it was right here.

'It was a totally different kind of war but our troops once again proved their mettle. They adapted to the situation in an instant and did excellent work in tandem with the trackers of the Tsumeb farm commando.'

When the operation was over, the troops returned to the mushrooming base under the camelthorn trees. Soon, 61 Mech would leave Omuthiya in force once again – this time to take the war to the enemy in Angola.

Platoon 1, Bravo Company, was like a little United Nations, Marco Caforio likes to joke. In an army dominated by Afrikaners they were a mixed bunch: 'Souties, Italians like me, Greeks, some boertjies of course … all sorts.'

---

1 The attacks on the farms in the grimly nicknamed 'Driehoek van die Dood' (Triangle of Death) are described in my book *Tannie Pompie se Oorlog*.

On 8 May 1979, a group of Swapo insurgents invaded Wilderness, the Roodt family farm near Tsintsabis. Only the two youngest Roodt children, aged three and four, and their grandmother were at home. All were murdered. The insurgents then moved further south and murdered the elderly Adolf Friederich on his farm Tsutsab.

These were the bloodiest attacks on farmers in South West Africa up to that time. Dippenaar temporarily moved his tactical headquarters and troops to Tsumeb and took overall command of the counterinsurgency operation. Within two weeks, most of the insurgents were dead and the survivors had fled back to Angola. Dippenaar then focused his energy on completing the base at Omuthiya and forging 61 Mech.

When Marco reported for his two years' national service, he wanted to be a paratrooper, just like his paternal grandfather, who fought in World War II then relocated his family from a devastated Europe to South Africa.

During basic training at 1 SAI, the parabat recruiting officers came round and Marco went for it. He passed the initial selection and packed his *balsak* (kitbag) to move to 1 Parachute Battalion – virtually next door in the sprawling Tempe military complex – to try and earn his wings. There, he met Robert de Vito from Boksburg, who was also of Italian origin. Both dropped out during one of the gruelling evaluation phases, however, and got their 'RTU' (return to unit) orders. And back to 1 SAI they went.

By pure chance, they both ended up in Platoon 1, section 3. 'We became very close buddies, we had a lot in common. Suffered together during training and went jolling on weekend pass together … us and Andrew Madden from Benoni,' Marco relates in his Roodepoort home more than four decades later.

And eventually they arrived at Omuthiya together. Platoon 1, Bravo Company, moved into the sweating brown tents under the camelthorn trees.

One member of their platoon was having the time of his life in this new environment: HP Ferreira, the farm boy from Theunissen. He was assigned as the driver of Ratel 21 (the platoon commander's vehicle). But his fondest memory is of the lengthy patrols they did on the farms in the Tsumeb district.

Those farms were vast, he remembers, and it could take up to five days to patrol one properly. The farmers and their wives received the young soldiers with open arms: 'They would slaughter livestock when they heard we were coming and gave us great food, plenty of it. And they made sure we had comfortable cots to sleep on.'

Marco's friend Rob de Vito.

Rob de Vito (centre) during basic training at 1 SAI.

Too soon the days of peaceful driving and warm hospitality were over. Back at Omuthiya they once again fell into the endless routine of training and maintenance of vehicles and equipment. But HP was no slacker when it came to scavenging for those little luxuries that made every soldier's life more bearable.

'When a driver was needed for a supply run to Grootfontein I always volunteered. At Grootfontein we loaded big boxes of meat for the kitchens and, well, those storemen based there were a bit slow … All you had to do was chuck the boxes into the back of the truck so fast that they couldn't keep a proper tally. The same with tinned food and crates of beer for the canteen … That night, back at Omuthiya, we would have a lekker braai and chug some beers.'

The next morning there would be the inevitable opfok or 'bosbus' – chasing the platoon up and down the sandy road called the 'Witpad'. But for HP, who as a kid loved nothing better than to run like a gazelle over the farm, this was no deterrent.

The other guys deliberately ran in a tight knot and at a measured pace that the slowest guy in the platoon could maintain, ignoring the shouts of the corporal to get their arses into a higher gear. Just like seasoned troops do. But HP ran at full tilt and the others let him go, because that was his thing.

'I loved it because boy could I run. Sometimes I already had a shower by the time the other guys came jogging up to the tents.'

HP Ferreira, Marco Caforio, Gareth Rutherford from Kalk Bay, Jan Hoevers from Ermelo and the others were quite settled in Omuthiya by the time Paul Louw arrived as a brand-new 'one pip' (second lieutenant).

'We got there and the first thing you see are troops looking like real *oumanne*, their skins brown as leather, sun-bleached uniforms and sporting moustaches. And then I was given Platoon 1, a bit of a handful as rumour had it …'

A standard mechanised infantry platoon had four Ratels: one for the platoon commander and one for each of the three sections. Each section consisted of seven riflemen, the driver and the gunner who manned the Ratel's 20 mm cannon and 7,62 mm Browning machine gun, and was led by a section leader (two-stripe corporal).

In the platoon commander's Ratel you would usually find (apart from his driver and gunner) the 60 mm mortar team, the platoon signaller and medic, the platoon NCO (also a corporal) and the orderly.

As platoon commander of Bravo Company, Paul's radio call sign was 21 (two-one). His section 1 was 21A (also called Alpha section); section 2 was 21B (Bravo section); and section 3 was 21C (Charlie section). Each Ratel's call sign was painted on the hull in large numbers, so that everyone knew who travelled and fought in that Ratel. As a mechanised soldier, the call sign was part of your identity. It said where you belonged while you were wearing browns.

Paul held his corporals and lance corporals in high regard. Like Joe Lourens, from the mining town of Carletonville, who was in charge of section 1: 'Pappa Joe, we called him. He was a big, tough guy but very disciplined and a good section leader.'

When it comes to the ordinary troops, he dwells on section 3, 'a bunch of *Engelsmanne* and two Italians. They were a bit laid-back and sometimes did not realise the seriousness of things, but they were very good troops, all of them.'

On the one hand, you had big-city lads like Marco Caforio from Orange Grove, a Johannesburg neighbourhood where many immigrant families had settled. On the other, you had the farm boys from the Afrikaner-dominated platteland. On the surface of things they seemed worlds apart, but in the great melting pot of a mechanised war machine none of this mattered. They became buddies and true brothers-in-arms.

Crucial to the forging of the new unit was the training area in the bush about 15 km from Omuthiya. Countless hours were spent perfecting the tactics and drills of mechanised warfare: the attacking and defensive formations of Ratels on the move; the integration of infantry, armour and artillery; the critical moment when the order comes for troops to debus from their vehicles and assault enemy trenches on foot.

As they honed their combat skills, Paul's admiration for the young men placed under his command grew: 'They were the best of their intake by far. Damn good when it came to platoon and section fighting drills.'

He was sometimes criticised for 'getting too involved' with his troops. But he could not ask them to give their all if he remained aloof and distant, Paul argued: 'In the evenings I would visit them in their tents rather than hang out with the other lieutenants. It was important for me to get to know them and be there for them.

'I got them steaks to braai whenever there was an opportunity to do so. When I bought a bottle of brandy to share with the other officers, I also bought a bottle for each of my sections. But the next morning they had to be sharp and pull their weight at training or chores.'

He sometimes sensed that the other two platoons of Bravo Company were envious of the relationship he had with his men: 'Or maybe I imagined it. But damn, they were a lekker group of guys.'

And four decades later, Marco, one of the troops from his 'laid-back' section 3, returns the compliment: 'He was a great man, my lieutenant Paul Louw ... a good oke.'

Early in 1980, Bravo Company's routine and life at Omuthiya was interrupted by yet another chapter in southern Africa's long history of conflict.

They were driven south to Grootfontein in the large trucks dubbed 'Wit Olifante', and from there flown to the States. In Bloemfontein they were issued Ratels and from there travelled in convoy to Messina (today Musina), on South Africa's border with then Rhodesia.

Times were uncertain. With the Rhodesian bush war over, Robert Mugabe and his Zanu-PF party were about to participate in democratic elections for the first time. The apartheid government in Pretoria wanted a strong military force near the Beitbridge border post 'just in case'.

Jan Hoevers, who had waived the exemption that came with his former railways job in order to be the master of his own destiny, was now the driver of Ratel 21B. And on the road to Messina he learned how exhausting the long hours behind the wheel of a Ratel could be.

'In Potchefstroom we laid up for a few days and then the drivers were told to sleep during the day because that night we were going to drive the rest of the way to Messina (a distance of nearly 650 km). But it in the daytime heat it was impossible to sleep.'

Nevertheless, at 18h00 they started up and hit the road.

'After a time I was exhausted and asked the guys over the intercom to tell jokes or stories, whatever, just keep talking to keep me awake. But somewhere on the other side of Pretoria I just heard the sound of snoring from the back.'

The driver's chair and steering console is front and centre, just below the turret. Cramped, isolated and hot.

'You get used to how a Ratel handles, but the moment you

lose concentration you get that body roll, and then you have to straighten it out again. It's not like driving a car, and convoy driving is slow, so it gets boring.'

But he had to stay alert. A body roll could lead to an accident and injuries or death for the soldiers inside the Ratel. The lives of his sleeping buddies were in Jan's hands. The sun was rising by the time they arrived at the Messina municipal airport and started digging in on both sides of the runway.

Pretoria's fears of bloody mayhem during the elections on the other side of the border would prove unfounded. Paul Louw's biggest challenge was to keep his platoon busy and disciplined. And, as usual, Marco and his pals from the laid-back section 3 ruffled some feathers.

'In the mornings my platoon was supposed to eat breakfast first, followed by Platoon 2, Platoon 3, and so on. But every morning we ate last because section 3 was always late to fall in. Finally, big, scary Corporal Joe Lourens had enough. He came to me and said, "Lieutenant, I'm going to have to teach them to listen." And I told him to go ahead.'

Things came to a head the next morning: 'Our platoon had once again lost their prized spot at the head of the breakfast line. The other platoons had already eaten their fill but we were still waiting for section 3 ... Finally they came strolling out of the bush at their leisure.

'Big Joe strode towards them and started slapping them left, right and centre. By the time he got to the last one they were miraculously formed into a single file and running at the double. And that was the end of it; afterwards we always ate first!'

By the end of May 1980, they were on their way back to Bloemfontein, but not without mishap: 'We avoided the N1 and used the back roads. When we passed Welkom a guy on a bicycle got hit by a Ratel. From my own turret I saw a spray of blood in the air, a sight I'll never forget.'

But when you're in a moving convoy, you don't just hit the brakes.

'I reported it on the radio but was simply ordered to keep going; the military police and traffic officials would sort it out ... It seems scary but those sort of things happened.'

Finally, the 'borrowed' Ratels were returned to the big hangars at De Brug near Bloemfontein and Bravo Company was granted a week's leave before the flight back to the Border and Omuthiya. But there was one unusual condition, HP Ferreira remembers.

'Every evening we had to watch the final SABC news broadcast at seven o'clock ... Riaan Cruywagen was still the presenter back then. And if he said the code word at the end of the bulletin, we had to report for duty immediately.'

And, as fate would have it, their cherished leave was indeed cut short by the word 'Foxbat'. They hurried back to Bloemfontein, blissfully unaware that their baptism of fire was drawing closer.

HP's dad drove him and his pal Gertjie Kemp (the driver of Ratel 21A) from the farm to the petrol station outside the town of Theunissen. There, they would wait briefly under the road sign showing the silhouette of a hitch-hiking soldier. 'People never failed to stop at that sign. Within ten minutes you got a lift to Bloemfontein, every time.'

It was not the first time HP bade his father goodbye under that sign. But that day he heard himself say: 'Pa, I'll come home again. But when I come home, I won't be whole anymore.'

Back in Bloemfontein, he marched up the loading ramp of a Flossie with the rest of Bravo Company for the long flight to the

Border, his strange parting words already forgotten.

But all too soon he would have reason to recall that moment by the roadside before his dad drove off.

5

SECRET PLANS AND PREMONITIONS OF DOOM

The need to ensure the utmost secrecy was the biggest challenge during the planning and preparation for the assault on Smokeshell, Johann Dippenaar stresses.

'It's really difficult to put an operation like this together without anybody getting a whiff of what's going on. The secrecy also meant that the intelligence you received was not always as comprehensive, up-to-date or accurate as you needed it to be.'

Technology such as GPS navigation or Google Maps, so common today, did not exist in that era. The target was just a featureless patch of Angolan bush. Clandestine aerial photos, sparse information gleaned from prisoners and outdated Portuguese maps were just about all Dippenaar and his planning team had to work with. They had to figure out what they would be up against, plot the approach and assault routes, and work out the countless minute details of a battle plan.

'This was when I learned that the intelligence community, the guys who had to give you all the answers in order for you to plan your operation, could also get it wrong. They simply did not have enough information to work with … It was a very trying time.'

However, the SADF's analysts and top brass agreed on one thing: Swapo was mobilising for another big push into the South West African bush during the rainy season when denser foliage and seasonal water counted in its favour.

This time, Pretoria was determined to take the battle to Angola – far away from the vast farming districts of Otavi, Grootfontein and Tsumeb, collectively known as the Triangle of Death. By April 1980, the decision for a pre-emptive strike had been made.

But Swapo had also learned from its previous clashes with the SADF.

When Dippenaar accompanied Bestbier's assault force during Operation Reindeer in May 1978, the enemy positions were near the Angolan town of Ongiva. The area, well-known to the SADF, was only about 50 km north of the border and the terrain was open – ideal for a classic mechanised attack.

Swapo did not forget the lessons of Reindeer. It moved its command and logistical complexes deeper into Angola – in the case of Smokeshell, 180 km from the border – to make them less vulnerable to surprise raids. These locations were far from handy geographical references such as towns, buildings or tar roads. And, rather than concentrate its forces, Swapo dispersed them, using the protective dome of the bush as cover from prying eyes in the sky.

As a result, the intelligence provided to Dippenaar was flawed. Piece by piece, the puzzle was built, 'but the picture of what Smokeshell looked like was never quite clear. At best, we knew more or less where it was.'

What Dippenaar and his team managed to construct in their operations room under the camelthorn trees was an enemy complex spread over a swathe of bush 15 km long and 3 km wide and bristling with between 600 and 800 Swapo fighters in 13 sub-bases. Dippenaar recalls: 'Where do you start, and what do the approaches look like? There's no road to begin with, so how do you get within striking distance in the first place? How do you cross the border with your force? The challenges were immense.'

He was worried about the lack of clear answers, but time was running out. The window of opportunity for Smokeshell – May or June – was fast approaching. So he got his senior leadership team together and started grafting.

Another major headache was equipment and provisions. Many vehicle- and man-portable radios were needed because communications would be key. Weapons systems had to be tested properly and sufficient quantities of diesel, oils and lubricants, batteries, tyres, food rations and ammunition of all types would have to follow on the heels of the mechanised combat group.

And then there was the need to find the right men for the right job in this relatively new way of waging war – whether it be mechanised infantry, armour or artillery – and the logistics guys and tiffies to support a force of roughly 160 vehicles and 1 600 men over unforgiving terrain. For this was to be the greatest conventional onslaught by a South African force in Africa since World War II.

'There was absolutely no blueprint. In hindsight it was a miracle that we achieved what we did,' Dippenaar says.

Under the camelthorn trees the battle plan was revised time and again as new snippets of information came from Pretoria. It gave Dippenaar the opportunity to identify his strongest leaders: 'You could clearly see who had control over his own force, who grasped the bigger picture and contributed towards it, whether they were officers or non-commissioned officers [NCOs].'

Secrecy was a growing concern. How to get the troops prepared and razor-sharp without them guessing that something was up?

And around this time Dippenaar's long-awaited second company of mechanised infantry came rolling down the Witpad.

'You know, when those new troops are let loose in the bush they can get up to a lot of funny business. They don't know anything about war and a pending operation yet, but at the same time you have to get them ready or risk failure.'

For Dippenaar wanted the operation to succeed, but he also wanted his men to come home alive.

Secrecy or not, Paul Louw and the lads of Platoon 1 had a gut feeling that something big was brewing: 'There was that tension in the air and you just knew.'

They were ordered to dig trenches on the training site near Omuthiya, which they stormed to clear out the imaginary enemy: 'We went through those drills two, three times a week. The drivers had to learn to leap their Ratel over trenches and we did trench clearing way beyond the point of boredom.'

During one such exercise they came across a stray warthog in a trench. The troops lost all interest in refining the art of war and gave chase, for roast warthog would be a welcome change from the usual army fare. They succeeded in getting their meal, but Bravo Company's new commander – Captain Louis Harmse, who had just replaced the much-loved Cassie Schoeman – was not amused, Paul recalls.

Each day's training was followed by vehicle and weapons maintenance by the drivers and gunners. Changing Ratel wheels in the field was hard work, and the riflemen of every section had to practise lifting the huge spare wheels onto the roof of the vehicle with all possible speed.

The rumour mill was working tirelessly. On 31 May, ten days

before the planned attack date, Dippenaar decided to confirm what everybody suspected. He assembled the unit in the big open-sided mess hall and told them: You're going on an operation in enemy territory. This is what you're going to do.

'He was short and to the point,' recalls Lance Corporal Gareth Rutherford, the medical orderly of Paul's section 2. (Medical orderlies, or 'combat medics', were fighting paramedics – the men who stabilised the wounded amid flying bullets until the choppers could get them out.)

Dippenaar's announcement was met with silence. Then he extended an unusual invitation: 'Those of you who do not feel up to it – because some will die – should stand back. I'm going to give you a bit of time but then you have to make up your minds.'

He did so, Dippenaar says, because he wanted each troopie to know exactly what he was letting himself in for. Every man had to decide whether he was willing to give his all and fight as part of a team.

'And nobody stood back. All of them said they wanted to go. For me, that was one of the requirements to succeed.'

But there's a kink here. Corporal Paul Kruger, who was in charge of Marco Caforio's 'laid-back' section, approached Paul Louw and asked not to go.

Kruger was a member of the Springbok gymkhana team. 'There was to be a tournament in East London and he had actually requested leave to participate even before the operation in Angola was announced,' Louw explains.

'But by that stage the security around the operation was in place and he was simply told: "You don't have to go to Angola, but we can't risk you leaving the base. So you'll have to stay at Omuthiya and miss your gymkhana tournament anyway."'

Kruger chose to go with the men of his section.

After Dippenaar's brusque announcement, training for the assault continued. He also used models of the objectives, which were as accurate and close to scale as could be managed.

'Every afternoon, for two or three hours, every guy who would play a leadership role of some sort had to use a model to explain what he was going to do,' explains Dippenaar. 'Every man had to know exactly what was expected of him – and if things did not turn out as expected, what was he going to do, what was the alternative? You had to get your leader group to buy in to the fact that this is the real thing, this is war.'

The same went for the troops. 'They got our blood up and made us excited,' Gareth Rutherford relates. 'We were told we were going to be part of something very big and important, but also dangerous.'

And it struck a chord at the time. In his diary, Gareth wrote that he would be proud to die while defending his country. But rereading that entry 42 years later in his Swellendam home, he takes a playful dig at his 18-year-old self: 'Now that's brainwashing and propaganda for you!'

They were also told about the enemy's 'gruesome-looking anti-aircraft guns'. Their long twin barrels seemed like vampire teeth to Gareth. The rounds from the guns could 'chow Ratels like a hot knife through butter', he had heard – and his platoon's job was to destroy four of them.

Thoughts about vampire-toothed guns did not deter him from indulging in a last feast on the eve of departure for Angola: 'Pork chops, rice, tea and potatoes, followed by a couple of peanut butter and apricot jam sandwiches for dessert. They were bulking us up for the fighting to come.'

He packed, repacked and checked the contents of his medical bag over and over. Needles, drip bags, wound powder, morphine, field dressings …

In section 3's tent, right next door, Marco Caforio had a bone-chilling experience: 'I think it was the night of 7 June when we had a bit of a piss-up. We knew we were going on this big operation so we asked our lootie, Paul Louw, to organise us a bottle of rum. We listened to Pink Floyd while we drank and talked about this big, unknown thing that we were heading into.'

Robert de Vito sat next to him on one of the metal army cots, just like they, as riflemen 3 and 4 of their section, always sat next to each other in the Ratel or went through ground combat drills shoulder to shoulder. Best friends and brothers-in-arms.

'All of a sudden Rob nudged me and said: "Marco, I don't know if I'm going to make it." And I said, "Rob, what are you talking about?" And then he said, "I don't know, but this operation is going to be a big thing in my life."

'I told Rob not to talk like that. We're going to do what we were trained for and then we're going to come back from Smokeshell. And that was when he said: "Promise me you'll always stay in touch with my family." I told him not to talk kak, but he kept on asking me until I promised that I would.'

Marco ('We Italians are a superstitious bunch, you know, we're a bit weird that way') noticed more unusual behaviour among his mates of the 'United Nations'.

'You know, Andrew Madden never used bad language, but that night he changed … he started swearing like a sailor. All these years later I still get the chills when I think of it.'

Meanwhile, Jan Hoevers was 'sort of psyched up. You've been training for this for so long and you're ready for it. It's not like an exam when you worry, did I study enough of this or that? You've been trained and you knew what to do, you just had to go do it.'

He claims not to be the superstitious type. But once the fighting and dying was over, Jan would have cause to remember the odd behaviour of some guys on the eve of their departure for Smokeshell.

'One of the guys said: "You can have my coffee and sugar, because I'm not going to come back." I thought it strange, because your coffee and sugar were just about the only personal stuff you had. Everything else belonged to the army.'

The guy who gave away his sugar and coffee would indeed not make it back. 'And there were a few others who said they were afraid, that they knew they would not return. At the time you thought: "Ag, what does he know?" But some of them were right after all, it's so heartbreaking.'

And then 8 June dawned and the endless and obsessive preparations were over. After a few hours of restless sleep, they assembled for scripture and prayer and then it was time to mount up and go.

Dippenaar's attack force comprised three combat teams and each of these was assigned specific targets in the complex of bases collectively dubbed Smokeshell. In effect, it would be a near simultaneous, three-pronged ground assault. Puma helicopters would drop parabats behind the enemy to cut off their escape routes.

Bravo Company, led by Captain Louis Harmse and including Paul Louw's platoon, was the mechanised infantry component of Combat Team 2.

Omuthiya was conveniently close to the good tar road that ran in a northwesterly direction up to the Angolan border. Close to the border there was a turnoff to the east and Eenhana (the SADF base where Dippenaar planned to cross). But, because of the need for secrecy, the wheels of Dippenaar's fighting force – infantry, armour and artillery – were not going to be kissed by tar: 'There was an obscure dirt track that ran from Omuthiya to the north and that's the way we went … straight north, up to where we had to turn west to Eenhana.' This would be a longer and tougher route, however, and would require an overnight halt.

The long convoy was divided into 'packets'. The vanguard left Omuthiya at 10h00 on 8 June and the others followed at regular intervals.

To get a large convoy, consisting of different vehicle types, from one point to another over difficult terrain is a gruelling affair. It takes good planning, proper command and control, and discipline – even before the shooting starts.

For the young national service drivers, it was a gruelling day's work. The great wheels of the heavy vehicles soon demolished the sandy track. The convoy was swallowed by a cloud of Ovamboland dust as fine and white as Johnson's baby powder. The dust impaired vision, and drivers had to concentrate hard in order not to rear-end the vehicle in front.

In the stifling-hot troop compartments of the Ratels, some riflemen dozed with lolling heads while the turbo diesel engines sighed and whined, only to jerk awake when a wheel bumped through a pothole.

The tail end of the convoy had the worst of it. Big echelon vehicles laden with rations, ammunition and other essentials got stuck in the soft sand, as did the 'gun tractors' towing artillery pieces.

The first vehicles arrived at their overnight destination, Oshifitu, at around 15h00 and the last at 20h00. Here they were refuelled, the tiffies did running repairs and cargo was resecured after the bumpy ride. Troops cleaned their rifles, brewed a quick coffee and washed away the dust of the road as best they could before crawling into their sleeping bags.

The next morning, 9 June, they started up again and turned to the west for the last 75 km to Eenhana, where the head of the convoy rolled in around 15h00. Here the respite would be even briefer because the plan was to cross into Angola as soon as the cloak of darkness fell.

At Eenhana, 61 Mech was joined by the two parabat companies in their open-topped, swaying Buffel troop transports, and by a special guest – General Constand Viljoen, Chief of the Army. Viljoen was going to hitch a ride to Smokeshell in Dippenaar's command Ratel, call sign Zero.

At 18h30 Dippenaar convened his core leadership group: 'There at Eenhana we stood on a dune and, one more time, made sure that everybody knew what they had to do.' Half an hour later, as the shroud of night started to cover the landscape, he gave the order to start up and go. Over the border and into Angola.

Gone was the bravado and nervous energy of the preceding days. He could sense the tension running through his force: 'There was no turning back anymore. I think if I had waited until that moment to ask if any of the guys wanted to stay behind, a few may have done so … because just then the reality really hit home.'

6

BLOOD AND FIRE IN THE BUSH

The choreography of the attack – where and when each of Dippenaar's three combat teams would peel away from the main force in order to strike their designated targets – also dictated the marching order when they crossed into Angola.

Combat Team 3 would attack the north side of the sprawling Swapo complex and Combat Team 1 the centre. Combat Team 2, with Paul Louw's platoon at the tip of the spear, would hit the south side.

But first they had to grind on through most of the night to Mulemba in Angola, where they would consolidate for the final thrust to Chifufua and Smokeshell.

There was no road to speak of, just a barely visible track through the bush. Sparsely detailed maps, a handheld compass and the Southern Cross were the only navigational aids – as they were for the mariners who first found their way to this former Portuguese colony in Africa.

At times the Ratels had to 'bundu bash', meaning the leading vehicle smashed a path through the brush using its weight and power. The other vehicles stuck to the freshly made wheel tracks while each driver kept an eye on the single red navigation light on the rear of the preceding vehicle. Using headlights while on enemy turf was a bad idea.

This worked fine for a number of Ratels travelling in single file at, say, 20 km/h. But the wheel track width of an Eland armoured car, for instance, was narrower than that of a Ratel and they battled to keep up. At times, progress slowed to a mere 10 km/h.

If you see an elderly man driving his car with the palms of his hands pressed against the steering wheel and fingers splayed open, you may well be looking at a former Ratel driver. Because if you clamped your fingers around the steering wheel and hit a big tree root, the shock could break your wrist. Or so the story goes.

The border crossing was an anticlimax for Paul Louw and his platoon. You drive over the cutline, just a sand road really, and that's that. No enemy in sight. One reason for this was that a raiding force prefers not to announce its arrival by using a formal border post. Besides, the immigration officials with their passport stamps had abandoned their stations long ago.

Paul's platoon was sent ahead 'because we had the task to prepare landing spots at Mulemba so the choppers could refuel. So we drove through the night, and when we got there we chopped down some small trees and flattened the rest with the Ratels. Pretty soon we had a big enough open spot for the choppers to land.'

The plan was that the parabat 'stopper' groups would accompany the rest of the convoy to Mulemba in their Buffel troop carriers to rendezvous with the Puma helicopters. After refuelling, the Pumas would airlift the parabats to their ambush positions behind the enemy fortifications at Smokeshell. The big birds and their human cargo would be escorted by a number of 'gunships' – smaller, more agile Alouette helicopters armed with 20 mm automatic cannons. The precious avtur (aviation fuel) would also arrive with the convoy.

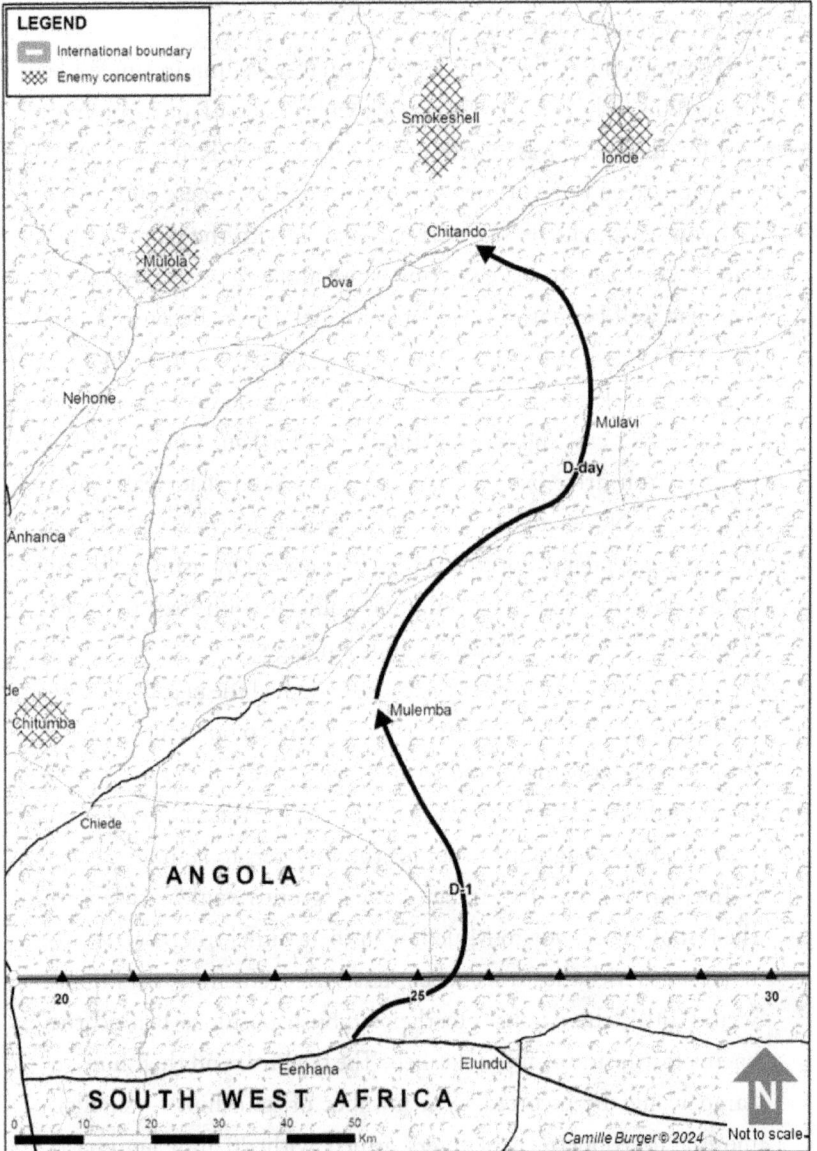

LEGEND
- International boundary
- Enemy concentrations

The advance from Eenhana in South West Africa to Smokeshell in Angola.

With their task completed well before daybreak, Platoon 1 could crawl into their sleeping bags to snatch a few hours of rest. Marco, however, could not shake off his uneasiness. He walked over to where Rob de Vito was standing guard and offered to take his place. But his friend said: 'No, Marco, you go sleep. I want to smoke and look at the stars.'

But Rob never smoked before, Marco recalls: 'Everything was changing. Guys who never smoked did so that night or acted differently in other ways. It was like the pieces of a puzzle clicking into place. Something was about to happen.'

The rest of the convoy arrived piecemeal – but without the chopper fuel. Somebody had buggered up and it remained south of the border. Now there was not enough aviation fuel for the Pumas and their gunship escorts. The air force refused to airlift the parabats into position. Dippenaar and the parabat commander were furious, but there was nothing to be done.

Then it was time to mount up for the final advance and assault on Smokeshell. The date was 10 June and D-day had dawned.

Before the engines roared into life, every man received a specially printed motivational card from Dippenaar. It bore the insignia of his new unit – the number '61' and a slanted lightning bolt in red – and the words from St Paul's Second Epistle to Timothy: 'As for you, my son, be strong through the grace that is ours in union with Christ Jesus.'

And in bold black letters: '**Now is the time!!**'

Dippenaar's account of that final advance, the battle and the aftermath was thoroughly documented in *Mobility Conquers: The Story of 61 Mechanised Battalion Group 1978–2005*, by Willem Steenkamp and Helmoed-Römer Heitman (commissioned by the 61 Mech Veterans Association). Some things, however,

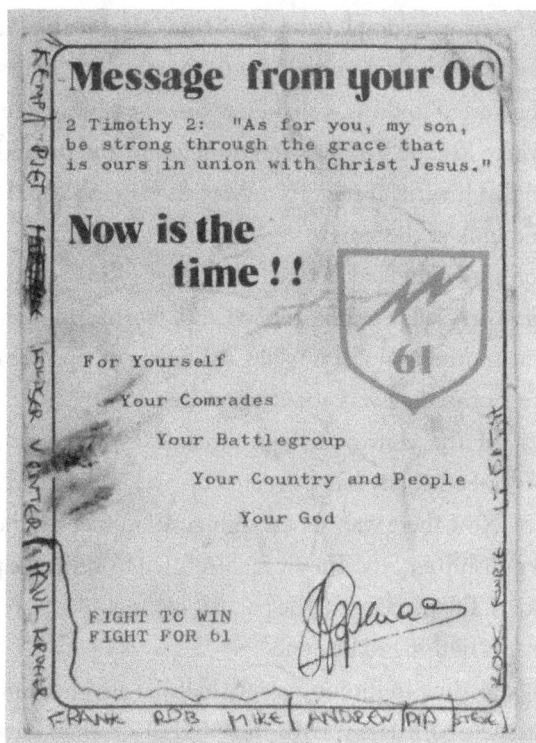

The motivational card distributed by Dippenaar to his men.
Gareth Rutherford wrote the names of the dead on his.

cannot be overstated. During Operation Reindeer in 1978, Frank
Bestbier could see his entire mechanised force while they attacked
over relatively open terrain. Dippenaar never enjoyed that key
advantage. His force was split into three combat teams dispersed
to attack over a vast area. And the bush at Smokeshell was much
thicker, impeding visibility and mobility.

His crucial role, from the turret of Ratel Zero, was overall
command and control. To deploy, consolidate and redeploy his
available forces in real time as the fluid battle raged. And, equally

important, to impose calm in this world of chaos and adrenaline-filled radio voices.

But four decades later in his sunny living room in Pretoria, he stresses that his eyes could not see where the anti-aircraft fire was punching holes through the Ratels of Paul's platoon: 'I can only talk about my part. What those guys experienced in that moment and spot, only they can tell you. I only heard about the fire they were taking. You see the billows of black smoke and you know that is not a tree burning, that is a vehicle burning. The reality of it hits you hard, but what do you do? You do your job, and my job was to keep control of the entire force.'

Let us, then, give voice to a few men of Platoon 1, Bravo Company, who survived that hellish day of fire and blood – a day that changed their lives for ever.

PAUL LOUW, RATEL 21

Witgoud (toilet paper) and slash marks on tree trunks left by two Recces showed Platoon 1 the way. 'We basically followed a straight line north, but we had to bundu-bash a lot; we made a new road through the bush,' Paul recalls.

But when you do a lot of bundu-bashing, small twigs and leaves fall into the Ratel and find their way everywhere, something that caused serious problems when the shooting started. Says Paul: 'Most of my platoon's 20 mm cannons malfunctioned because, no matter what we did, some of this gunk found its way into the mechanisms.'

They pushed on regardless because they had to be on the assembly point for the attack by 14h00. Overhead, a Bosbok light reconnaissance aircraft guided them to their objective 'until Swapo started pouring fire at the Bosbok and drove it away'.

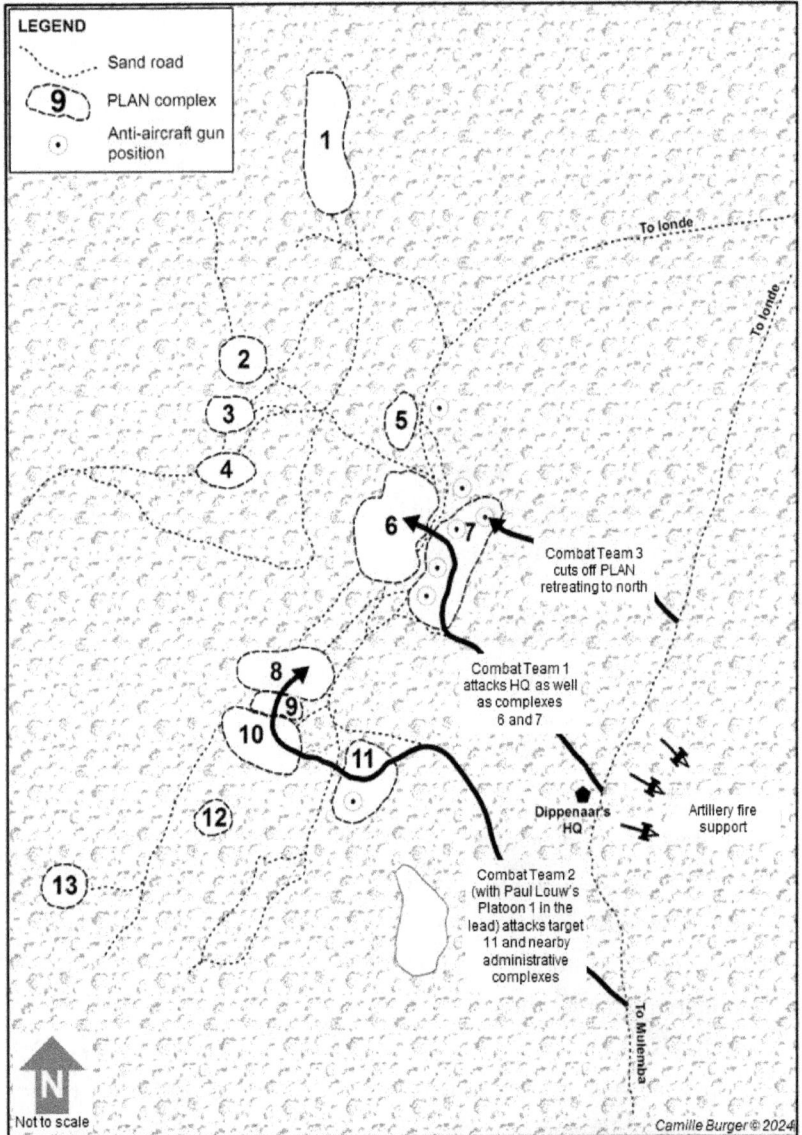

LEGEND
- Sand road
- 9 PLAN complex
- Anti-aircraft gun position

1

To Ionde

To Ionde

2

3

4

5

6 7

Combat Team 3 cuts off PLAN retreating to north

Combat Team 1 attacks HQ as well as complexes 6 and 7

8

9

10

11

12

13

Dippenaar's HQ

Artillery fire support

Combat Team 2 (with Paul Louw's Platoon 1 in the lead) attacks target 11 and nearby administrative complexes

To Mulemba

N
Not to scale

Camille Burger © 2024

The plan for the attack on Smokeshell. Combat Team 2 (with Paul Louw's Platoon 1 to the fore) hits the south.

They were on their own. But the layout of the objective and the attack plan were etched into his memory thanks to Dippenaar's scale models and countless tests: 'We knew more or less where our objective was. When we found a north–south road, that was our assembly point. From there we were to attack from east to west. So if we drove towards the west, we would find our objective.'

Each of the 13 targets at Smokeshell was assigned a number by Dippenaar and his planning team. Platoon 1's target was Number 11, 'a vehicle park for Swapo's troop carriers and trucks, as well as three anti-aircraft gun positions'.

Paul's orders were simple: 'Fight through the objective, destroy the enemy, vehicles and guns, regroup and await further orders.'

But the layout as shown by the aerial photographs provided to Dippenaar was not accurate. Or possibly Swapo decided to move its positions after an ineffective South African Air Force bombing raid just days before the planned ground assault. (Dippenaar was neither consulted nor informed.)

Bottom line: things were not as expected. The trenches and bunkers were deep and well protected and so were the fearsome ZU-23-2 guns. And, contrary to predictions, the enemy would put up a hard fight.

Platoon 1 was about to get a terrible surprise – but first there was yet another setback.

Earlier, during that morning's hard drive to Smokeshell, Captain Louis Harmse's Ratel suffered a broken accelerator. He promptly commandeered the Ratel of his second-in-command, Lieutenant Hannes du Toit. The frustrated Hannes could only look on as his own vehicle raced after the rest of Bravo Company with Harmse in the turret, while he remained behind with Harmse's stricken Ratel.

There would be a downside to this episode for Paul. As a young and untried junior officer, he would have to make life-or-death decisions in the heat of the battle without the guidance of his more experienced company commander. But more about that later.

Up front, Paul had reached the point where the final attack was to start: 'Over the radio I heard Commandant Dippenaar's order, "Laat waai!" and we started moving.'

The four Ratels moved in extended line through the bush, never more than 50 m apart, but even then visual contact was difficult: 'We kept going and going and started drawing sporadic small arms fire ... small skirmishes here and there ... but nothing big.'

The expected enemy vehicle park and gun positions were nowhere to be seen. There were just a few old trenches and fake gun positions fabricated from tree trunks and canvas.

Paul's legs suddenly felt tired, whether from the long hours standing in the turret or a sudden drop in adrenaline, and he sat down to take a breather. The move saved his life. For, as his head sank below the level of the hatch, a bullet, 'probably from an AK-47', smacked into the armoured glass of his observation block – a thick, brick-shaped window. 'If I hadn't sunk back into the turret at that exact moment it would have hit me between the eyes.'

The Ratels moved through their supposed objective from east to west. But there was still only light resistance. Where was the bulk of the enemy? 'Then we crossed a dim, sandy track and I saw a dry riverbed directly ahead. According to our maps, that riverbed was at the far side of our objective ... It could only mean we'd missed the objective.'

At this crucial moment, he had no radio communication with his company commander. For after Harmse commandeered his second-in-command's Ratel, he drove into a red-hot ambush. In the heat of the action the driver collided with a stout tree and the vehicle suffered a bent axle. Harmse then commandeered yet another Ratel and pushed on, but the vehicle radio was not tuned to the correct wavelength – meaning he could not communicate directly with Paul and his other platoon commanders.

Paul decided to go and find his target. He led his Ratels into the dry riverbed and turned north. But after proceeding a mere 500 m or so, he looked to his right and saw streaks of smoke belching from the barrels of Swapo's anti-aircraft guns.

What they were firing at he could not guess, but the smoke indicated the guns were about a kilometre east of Paul's position. The objective was there after all – just not quite where the aerial photographs said it would be – and well dug in and defended to boot. The preceding air raid and artillery barrage had done little to soften it up, but this Paul and his platoon did not know.

There in the riverbed he ordered his corporals to 'stap uit' (debus) from the Ratels, form up their sections and advance on foot. See where the enemy was then act as the situation demanded.

But, in an instant, he changed his mind. 'I said no, forget about leaving the vehicles for now, let's drive up and out of the riverbed and then plan our next move.'

Many years later, he would still berate himself for not doing reconnaissance on foot first or ordering his 60 mm mortar team to lob a speculative shell or two in order to flush out the enemy. Many others believe he's too hard on himself for a decision he made as a young, untried one-pip loot.

It was quite a steep climb out of the riverbed and Paul shouted into his radio mic for all vehicles to 'gee vet', to go up the bank at some speed in order to gain sufficient momentum. They did so in line abreast: Ratel 21C (section 3) on the far left; then 21A (section

1); then Paul's Ratel 21; and on the far right 21B (section 2). When they topped the river bank they were moving at about 50 km/h, Paul reckons.

And then they charged straight into hell.

The Soviet-made ZU-23-2 automatic cannon deployed by Swapo at Smokeshell earned its fearsome reputation in conflicts around the world.

It was light and robust enough to be towed over rough terrain. Wherever troop carriers and light trucks with off-road capabilities could go, so could these implements of death and destruction. They were easy and fast to deploy and operate. The guns were fed by ammunition belts housed in attached metal drums. The twin barrels spat the large rounds at a nightmarish rate and the open sights were simple but effective.

But what truly made the ZU-23-2 formidable was its versatility. In the classic anti-aircraft role the barrels were elevated almost vertically. But they could be lowered to the horizontal to blast away at ground targets. Compared to an aircraft, a Ratel was a big and slow-moving target – and too lightly armoured to withstand the 23 mm rounds.

What awaited Platoon 1 once they emerged from the dry riverbed was one of these terrifying cannons. Worse, it was protected by three 14,5 mm machine guns entrenched in a large triangle around their 'big brother'. (The 14,5 mm could also punch through a Ratel's armour). And protecting all these gun positions were foot soldiers in trenches and bunkers.

Straight into this hornet's nest charged Paul and his platoon.

For a long moment time stood still. The Swapo infantry and

gunners were as startled as the South Africans, Paul recalls: 'But there were hundreds of them and only 44 of us.'

Some seemed to run, but soon small arms fire was crackling like a veld fire around the Ratels. Only the 23 mm and the 14,5s remained silent: 'They were set up to fire towards the west but we came from behind, from the east.'

The textbook was now well and truly out the window. Leaving the Ratels and fighting forward on foot, as they were so well drilled to do, was not an option just then. They were in the heart of the enemy position and they had to push through. The troops fired their R1 rifles through the firing ports lining both sides of the hull or tossed hand grenades through the open hatches above their seats.

HP Ferreira, behind the steering wheel of Ratel 21, saw a Swapo sharpshooter in a tree and instinctively swerved to smash down the tree and crush its occupant.

Ratel 21A was the first to suffer a mortal blow when an RPG-7 warhead hit the driver's front window. 'Kempie, the driver, was hit by splinters in the face ... I believe he was blinded immediately and some glass splinters and other shrapnel probably entered his brain,' Paul says.

The RPG-7 rocket launcher was another feared weapon. It was light and portable enough to be fired by one man concealed in the bush, simple to maintain and use, and devastating to the men packed into the confines of a Ratel.

'Kempie' was Gertjie Kemp, who had joined HP on the family farm near Theunissen during that last brief stint of leave before they returned to the Border.

Then, at a range of only about a hundred metres, the 23 mm and 14,5s opened up, and the men of Bravo Company were in a world of fire and blood.

GARETH RUTHERFORD AND JAN HOEVERS, RATEL 21B (BRAVO SECTION)

Turning the yellowed pages of his diary, Gareth again seeks confirmation from the words he penned so long ago. The lined pages bear the symbol of the Southern Cross, revealing that it came from one of the tens of thousands of gift parcels handed to troopies by well-meaning tannies – many of them the wives of senior SADF officers or National Party officials.

'It felt like the earth and bush radiated anger. The bush got thicker ... then we veered to the right in line abreast and somebody shouted, "There's one" and our 20 mm and Browning opened up.' (The Browning 7,62 mm machine gun was mounted co-axially, next to the 20 mm cannon, in the Ratel turret and was the vehicle's secondary armament.)

'Through our sight blocks we saw hundreds of terrs looming up in the bush as we drove and we could hear the AK-47 rounds clattering against the hull.'

Jan Hoevers, the driver of 21B, glanced at his watch when he heard the first whip-like crack of an R1 rifle: 'It was three minutes past twelve. Then the order to cease fire came through the radio headset and I thought: "What the hell for, the enemy's right here?" But a moment later the order was reversed and everybody started blasting away.'

The Ratels soon filled up with acrid smoke and Gareth and his buddies were deafened by the sound of their own firing. Red-hot cartridge cases flew around the confined space as they were ejected from rifles.

'Then I shot my first one. I saw him stagger back and as his hat flew off my memory took a photograph of his face ... Madness took hold of us and we chucked M26 hand grenades

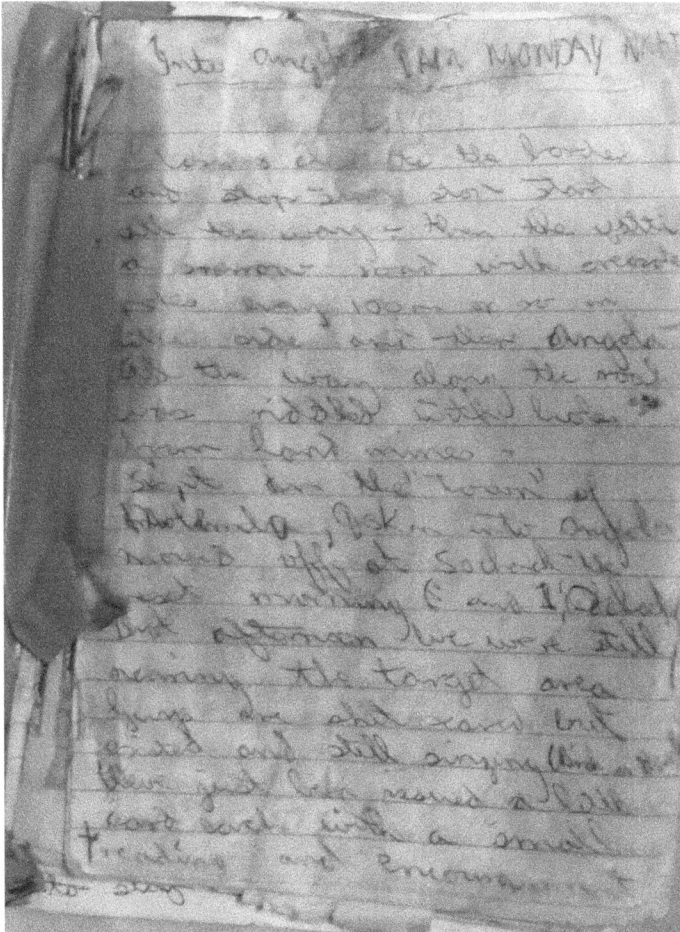

A page from Gareth Rutherford's war diary, in his own hand.

like automatons as enemy trenches flashed past.'

From his driver's seat, Jan saw an enemy soldier with an RPG-7 rocket launcher fleeing in front of him: 'My only thought was that if I drove past him, he was going to take us out with that thing from behind. I remember shouting at Willem, my back-up driver:

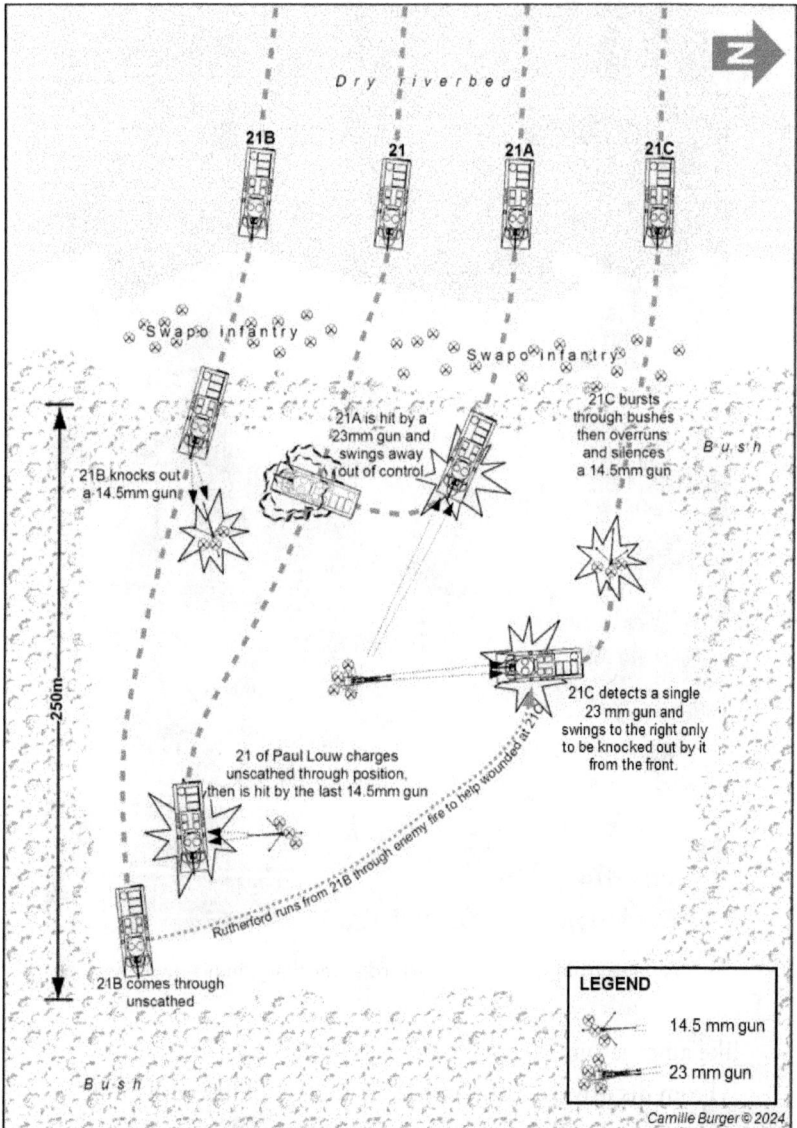

The destruction of three of Platoon 1's Ratels by Swapo's 14,5 mm machine guns and 23 mm anti-aircraft gun.

"I'm going to get him!" I chased him down and I remember he looked over his shoulder at me with huge, fearful eyes, then he stumbled and I was over him.'

All these years later, in the mock castle he built for himself high on a bluff overlooking Great Brak River, Jan pauses to reflect: 'You know, I felt this surge of excitement ... I could never have imagined that killing a human being by driving over him would excite me. It was just pure adrenaline, I reckon.'

Later Jan was told that he also drove over a second Swapo fighter. 'But I never saw a second guy. They said he was concealed under a bush.'

Fortune favoured Jan and his section that day, but not the Ratel on their flank.

'I saw my best friend Gert Kemp, in 21 Alpha, was on the wrong side of me. He was driving where I should be ... and then he got hit first, right through his driver's window. Bloody hell.'

Behind Jan, in the adrenaline-crazed troop compartment of the Ratel, Gareth remembers laughing at the confused expression of a mate who threw two grenades without remembering to pull the arming pins: 'He kept shouting: "Why won't the bloody things explode?"'

Then everything changed. Gareth felt their Ratel turn and he realised they had passed their objective and were heading back for another go.

'We were standing up in the open hatches and then we heard it: thunderous automatic fire. Something huge shooting and it sure as hell wasn't ours. And in that moment, you know it's tickets if that thing hits you. Everybody was terrified.'

Then the familiar command to 'stap uit' came over the internal radio speaker.

'We sure as hell did not want to, but the vehicle stopped and the doors hissed open. And then we did everything according to the book, just as we were trained to do. The Ratel started reversing while Vos, our gunner, laid down overhead covering fire and we sprinted away.'

For a fleeting moment he wondered why he did not see the other sections of Platoon 1 leave their own vehicles to form skirmish lines. Why where they hesitating?

What he did not know was that death was already reaping its grim harvest among the other sections. Soon after Gert Kemp was hit in 21A, Paul's Ratel 21 was also hit.

But the highest price of Smokeshell would be paid by the 'United Nations' – Marco Caforio and his buddies in Charlie section.

MARCO CAFORIO, RATEL 21C (CHARLIE SECTION)

He never could shake off that feeling of impending doom.

When recalling the events of 10 June 1980, Marco often refers to the superstitious nature of Italians. And he believes he had a guardian angel that day.

His Italian grandfathers fought in World War II: one as a paratrooper and the other – on his mother's side – as a marine in the fascist San Marco Battalion. And it was the latter who arrived in South Africa with Marco's parents in 1956.

At home they used to watch as the names of the Border War fallen scrolled down the television screen, Marco explains. 'And my grandfather would always say: "God must take me rather than my grandson." On 8 June, the day we left Omuthiya for Angola and Smokeshell, my grandfather suffered a heart attack and died. So that's why I believe I had a guardian angel.'

Pink Floyd's 'Another Brick in the Wall' was playing in the Ratel when they left Mulemba on the morning of the attack. But during that last advance they soon suffered a setback: 'I don't know what we hit, but the rear axle [the six-wheeled Ratels have three axles] broke. We were left stranded while the rest of the platoon kept going.'

Soon, vehicles from further back in the convoy came up to them. It was decided that Marco and his section would transfer to Ratel 9G (Nine-Golf), so 9G effectively became call sign 21C. They scurried to transfer all the extra ammunition and other necessities of war to their borrowed Ratel before setting off after their platoon. All the while Marco's unease was growing: 'I told Rob [de Vito] something's not right.'

They got to the supposed target area, where Paul and the others had passed through shortly before, and briefly left the Ratel to check out the trenches: 'But there was nothing, they were deserted. We saw no signs of damage from an air raid, no smoke, no movement in the surrounding bush. Nothing. We got back into the Ratel but suddenly the whole vibe had changed, all the okes were quiet now.'

Then, like Paul just ahead of them, they heard the tearing sound of a large cannon and, following the freshly made tracks of the other vehicles, caught up just in time for the charge up the river bank.

'We went over and drove into an old maize field and then they were everywhere, just as surprised as we were. Some were having lunch and they simply left their mess tins full of food on the lips of the trenches. I started shooting and somebody shouted, "Stop, wait for the command," but I thought bugger that and, like everybody else in our Ratel, carried on shooting.'

He was shaking, Marco recalls, as he realised this was it, 'the real thing'. But he and Rob, shoulder to shoulder as they had always been during training, alternately squeezed off shots and tossed grenades as fast as they could. (Below the sight blocks along the sides of the hull were individual firing ports allowing them to fire their rifles from inside the vehicle. But to throw grenades, the riflemen had to use the hatches on top of the hull, briefly exposing their heads and upper bodies to enemy fire and flying shrapnel.)

A grenade hurled by Martin French apparently detonated a Swapo ammunition pile: 'We felt the ground shake and heard WHUMP! WHUMP! WHUMP! as more stuff exploded. Martin grinned at me in triumph and shouted, "Hey, Marco!"'

He felt the Ratel churn around and suddenly the maize field they had just ploughed through was ahead of them again. Then he, too, heard the demonic roar of the enemy cannon and in the same instant they were hit.

'It's like that scene in the movie *Saving Private Ryan*. You know something terrible is happening but the world has gone utterly silent, as if you've just turned deaf. I saw blood coming out of Steve Cronjé's mouth and ears and he tried to reach the hydraulic doors but collapsed dead before he could do so and I thought, "Fuck, what is going on, what is actually happening?" Your brain refuses to process it.'

But the unthinkable was happening: 'A shower of green sparks (enemy tracers) were passing through the Ratel, as if somebody was welding inside. I saw Pip [Peter Warrener] crawling from the turret but his leg was gone, and I thought again, "What the hell am I seeing?" And the others must be seeing it too, but why is nobody saying anything? It's like you're outside your own body, looking down at yourself and just waiting for your turn to be hit.'

Marco did not realise that he was already wounded: 'I later heard that one of our own hand grenades detonated inside the vehicle and the shrapnel tore into my hip and leg.'

A hole in the hull of the Ratel in which Marco Caforio was wounded and seven members of his section died.

An emotionally drained soldier on the Ratel in which seven members of Charlie section died.

He started shoving at Rob while screaming, 'Get out, get out, they're hitting us!' And somehow he got out himself.

'I don't know how, but we were fit and strong, you know. I went flying through the hatch above my seat like a fish out of a barrel and landed on my back on the ground next to the vehicle. I could feel pieces of shrapnel moving around in my flesh and cutting me every time I moved, and I was bleeding. It hurt like hell but the adrenaline must have helped … I was desperate to find Rob and tell him I was wounded.'

He didn't know that Rob would not be able to help … his friend and six others inside Ratel 21C were dead or dying.

PAUL LOUW

Everything was plunging into chaos at a heart-stopping rate and his boys, the troops he felt so privileged to lead, were getting chopped to bits.

Paul was aware that 21A was hit when it crossed in front of 21B. Then he saw 21C starting to turn after its first pass to have another go: 'But in doing so he turned his nose straight at that 23 mil and got hit with a burst from dead ahead.'

Moments later, disaster also struck Paul and his crew in Ratel 21: 'One of the 14,5 mil positions was somewhere to my left. As we passed it fired a burst … Seven rounds went through the Ratel, some passing through right behind my seat and through the big hopper radios.'

He was incredibly lucky not to be hit by that burst, but the rounds hit the ammunition in the bins inside the Ratel. 'Everything just started to blow up.'

Steve Loubser, his signaller, was killed instantly where he sat on the small folding seat next to the turret, and soon the inside of the Ratel was an inferno. The fire was fuelled by more exploding ammo and various combustibles. Black smoke billowed above the bush and was visible for miles.

'I shouted at my guys to get the hell out and leap into empty enemy trenches, to go into *rondom verdediging* [form a defensive perimeter].' He tried to grab his R1 from the rifle rack inside the door nearest to him, but the flames bit into his arm and he abandoned it.

In the driver's compartment, HP Ferreira pulled the lever that opened the two hydraulic side doors. Because the 14,5 mm hit them from the left, everybody tried to bail out through the right-hand door, HP explains, 'but three of the guys got killed when they leaped outside.'

In the midst of this carnage, somebody – Paul still has no idea who – had the courage and presence of mind to hurl a grenade at the Swapo gun position: 'It took out the gun and must have detonated their ammo dump, because when we cleaned up the position later we found the charred bodies of the gun crew.'

Paul knew the two Ratels flanking his had also been taken out, but there was no sign of section 2: 'They had to be behind the screen of the bush but I could not see or hear them. But I was sure they went straight past the outside perimeter of the enemy position and therefore were not hit.'

Outside his burning vehicle he told his surviving crew members: 'Stay here, defend yourselves, I'm going to find section 2.'

Then came one of many moments of horror that he would relive in his nightmares: 'As I looked up at my Ratel, I saw Vaatjie, my tail gunner, climbing out. And at that exact moment he was hit in the head and I saw the blood spray from the wound ... These are the kind of things that are burned into your memory for ever.'

Then Paul started running though the bush and flying bullets, unarmed and alone, to where he thought his hopefully still unscathed section 2 might be.

HP FERREIRA, RATEL 21

Yes, he was scared driving into battle: 'All I knew was I was right out in front and I had to turn left, and for the rest I had no idea what was going on. At that time I'd never seen a dead person and never aimed a weapon at a human being.

'But off we went and I kept driving until Paul told me we're getting close now – maybe 300, 400 metres – and all of a sudden I heard "tang, tang, tang" against the Ratel. But it was small arms fire and we went through the position and turned ... and then the shooting got really loud. It was those anti-aircraft guns.'

Even then, he felt safe in the Ratel 'because I was told this thing was designed to keep you alive. The front plate (protecting the driver's seat) was angled to deflect rounds. But I never realised those 14,5 and 23 mils would go through that armour plate like a hot knife through butter.'

He kept driving. 'Paul was shouting, "Go this way, go that way," and the hot brass ejected from our Browning machine gun was hitting my back because the cartridge bag was full. But the gunner was too busy firing to empty it.'

In the chaos he never noticed that a burst of automatic fire had torn through the Ratel right behind his driver's seat. 'I suddenly realised the Ratel was burning, and when we stopped I instinctively opened the doors.'

He remembers little of what happened next: 'The memories come and go. I remember old Loubsertjie was sitting slumped on that little folding seat fitted to the inside of the big side door. I could not see whether he was dead or alive so I just pushed him out.'

HP tried to clamber out through the hatch above his seat but it would not open. So he squirmed backwards through the narrow space next to the gunner's position and out the side door: 'I did not have a rifle or anything else. I remember I took cover in the trench with the others … Then I saw Paul sprinting away and I decided to follow him.'

Maybe HP did not hear the order to stay put, or maybe he acted out of pure instinct. Whatever the case may be, he was struck down as if by lightning.

'I stood up and started to run and, in that instant, I saw the guy manning the 14,5 looking right at me, aiming at me, and then I was lying on the ground.'

Those who witnessed it saw a fountain of blood bursting from his back. The armour-piercing 14,5 mil round hit HP on his coccyx and tore through his intestines and stomach.

'I did not realise right away that I was hit. Then there was the smell of burned flesh and the bitter taste of it in my mouth. It reminded me of the smell when our farm workers scorched the intestines and lungs of a butchered animal on an open fire … just like that.'

Moments later the pain started. Like a red-hot poker thrust through his body, he recalls: 'It was excruciating. And you don't know what's happening to you, I tried to move but my body would not.'

Much later he would hear he was also hit by four AK-47 rounds. 'I remember being dragged and tossed into a Ratel, I think it was Paul who picked me up and got me into a passing Ratel so they could get me out of there.'

Of that drive he recalls little, 'only the tang, tang, tang of the bullets against the hull. It must have been a good while later when I came to my senses again, but now I was outside, lying next to a Ratel. I had a very vague sense of my surroundings. Like watching a confusing movie, there's people running around and noise but you don't know what's going on.'

Of the seriousness of his wounds he knew nothing, and even less about the drama playing out on the battlefield where so many of his friends were dead or fighting for their lives.

Because of a bizarre mistake, he was officially listed as dead on that day's casualty report. But about that, and of the red faces it caused, he would learn only much later. Finally, he was loaded onto a chopper. It lifted off, veered sharply to the south and skimmed over the tree tops towards Oshakati, where the military surgeons would have a very busy day.

Smokeshell was over for HP. But the Free State farm boy who loved to run like the wind had a lifelong struggle ahead of him.

At this point, it is necessary to catch up with Lieutenant Hannes du Toit, the second-in-command of Bravo Company, whose Ratel was commandeered by Captain Louis Harmse.

When we last heard of Hannes, he had been left stranded with Harmse's wrecked Ratel 20 (Two-Zero) and crew. However, he was not content to cool his heels while waiting for the tiffies to pitch up. In *Mobility Conquers* (the annals of 61 Mech), Rifleman SJ Koen, the driver of Two-Zero, relates how he managed to jury-rig the broken accelerator cable: 'When you stepped on the pedal it took a full 30 seconds for the vehicle to react, but at least we could get moving again.'

When they were about to move off, they noticed for the first time that a big branch was stuck in one of the tyres, looking for all the world like a spear. But this was no time to change the wheel. They snapped it off level with the tyre, hoped for the best and got going. Somewhere in front of them the battle was on and they made haste as best they could to get there.

It seemed like only minutes before they drove past one of those dreaded ZU-23-2 guns. Their adrenaline levels shot through the roof but it remained silent because the gunners were dead.

A Swapo fighter loomed out of the bush but the 20 mil and the Browning jammed. Somebody shouted, 'Run him over!' and SJ promptly swerved and did so.

Then Hannes saw a bizarre sight: his own Ratel, 20A (Two-Zero-Alpha), standing forlorn with a broken axle. Of Harmse there was no sign, but the crew looked okay, so Hannes pressed on because, by the sound of things, the fighting ahead was getting heated.

And then, suddenly, they were in the midst of one of the sporadic ambushes that were being sprung all over the sprawling battlefield. Their solitary Ratel was drawing small arms fire from all sides. While SJ was trying to drive through it, Hannes crept out of the commander's turret, made his way to the Browning machine gun mounted on an anti-aircraft bracket at the rear of the Ratel and started hosing the bush.

Manning that Browning while under heavy enemy fire demanded bravery of the highest order. He had to stand up in the open hatch with his head and torso exposed while operating the gun. And he stood out like a sore thumb, highly visible from the ground.

How many boxes of Browning ammo Hannes went through, SJ had no idea: 'But suddenly I heard a voice through my radio headset: "He [Hannes] says his chest is burning, he's been hit four times."'

Hannes slumped back inside the Ratel and the crew tended to his wounds as best they could while SJ raced through the bush in search of proper medical help. During that frantic drive they had another narrow escape: 'something' told SJ to hit the brake and, at that instant, an RPG-7 warhead flashed past the Ratel's nose.

Finally they were back at the spot where they had passed 21A, with its broken axle. 'I was in such a state of shock that I drove straight into 21A,' SJ recalls.

For Hannes it was too late. He had succumbed to his wounds – the only 61 Mech fatality on the day who was not a member of Paul's Platoon 1, but no less a blow for Bravo Company.

He would be awarded the Honoris Crux for bravery posthumously – one of two 61 Mech members to receive the coveted decoration for their actions that day.

7

HEARTBREAK AND HEROISM

War is not like a Hollywood action movie. When the battle rages, your brain has to process what is happening in your area of responsibility and how to react, in real time and with no room for mistakes, because the lives of others depend on your decisions.

In this deadly dance, each has his role to play, whether you're the commandant or the lieutenant.

'I've always said the buck stops with me,' Johann Dippenaar says. 'There's just no other way to reason about it. There's nobody else you can ask at that moment. And then you just have to trust … That's why leadership is so important to me, right down to the level of Paul and his troops. They had to know what it was all about so that they could develop trust.'

Smokeshell would prove to be an extreme test.

'At times during the assault it felt as if you were losing control, simply because so many things were happening at the same time. Like when Jakes [Captain Jakes Jacobs, commander of Combat Team 3] attacked on the right, only to report there was no target there. He found some weapons systems and trenches but no enemy fighters.

'For me as a commander that was quite a shock to hear there was no target where you believed it would be. Does that mean your plan is going to fail? Where is the target now? And then you have to make fresh decisions based on new information as it becomes available to you.

'And the next moment Paul Fouché [major, commander of Combat Team 1] reports the opposite: he found a strong enemy contingent on the other side, where we believed they would be, so his fight was in full swing.

'But then Paul Louw's [Combat Team 2, on the left flank] incident happened and basically brought everything to a standstill. I just stayed calm and took control and told the air force: "Send us helicopters." I took control of the artillery and told them where to lay down fire. And that was my job, to bring everything to a stop and establish order … Command and control.

'The next thing was when Louis Harmse [Paul Louw's company commander] arrived at my command vehicle. He had left his troops and was in a state of shock. I just told him: "Get in here and calm down." So I assumed command of his part of the operation. It all comes down to leadership and leaders trusting each other. Louis Harmse came to me, he did not try and do something else, and it was the same with the other leaders on the field.'

Dippenaar replaced Harmse with Major Jab Swart, an engineer officer from his reserve force. Jab was sent off to the hot zone and did a solid job.

Dippenaar reflects: 'It all sounds so easy but in that situation and those conditions … you're in very thick bush, there's no landmarks, there's shooting all around you and reports of fatalities are coming in … On an emotional level it's traumatic. Some guys keep their heads and some guys lose it.'

Dippenaar also had a close shave.

'Late in the day I got my senior leadership together to proceed to the spot where we were going to go into laager [defensive position] for the night. While I was talking the enemy fired at my position [with an anti-aircraft weapon]. A branch just above my head was blown clean off and fell on the vehicle. It was a reminder that this was not child's play, it was a matter of life and death, and everything boils down to leadership.'

Up ahead, 19-year-old Paul Louw was ignorant of the bigger picture that Dippenaar was seeing. There was the shock of his dead and wounded troops to deal with, but he also had the living ones to think about while the firefight raged on. He had to keep his head like never before.

And for that Dippenaar gives him all due credit: 'There, in his own situational environment, Paul was looking at things from another angle. He was the leader there and he remained the leader until the very end. Whether he could have made any different decisions is not for me to judge, because only he was there and only he knows what happened there.'

MARCO CAFORIO

As the wounded Marco dragged himself off the ground next to Ratel 21C to find his friend Rob de Vito, 'I felt an explosion but I could not hear a thing. I saw part of Rob, his legs, lying on top of the Ratel and I thought, oh, okay ...'

Then he saw his friend's upper body lying on the ground. 'I went to him and shook him and shouted "Rob! Rob! Rob!"' But there was no life in Rob's wide-open eyes.

'Then I cracked and pushed myself up against the Ratel, I had no idea what the hell was going on. Then I heard Van der Vyfer, our tail gunner, shouting at me: "Caforio, take cover, they're shooting at you!"'

But he remained standing while small arms fire smacked against the hull: 'Your brain is gone, I was struggling to breathe. All I could think was, where's the rest of 61 Mech, I had to get to them, but how? You're shitting yourself. After what I just saw, I did not want to play the hero, I just wanted to survive, to get away from that place.'

Van again yelled at him to take cover, but Marco shouted back, 'Where're all the guys?' And Van answered in Afrikaans: 'Almal is fokken dood, almal is fokken dood!'

Hopping on his uninjured leg, Marco went around the nose of their vehicle and to his horror saw that Paul Louw's Ratel was alight: 'I could see one of the guys in his Ratel was also burning. That's when I told Van: "You know, we have to get the hell away from here."'

The army will make a man out of you, he had so often heard. But those back-slapping armchair warriors were not here in this place of total madness. So he and Van started to run.

'Luckily, we both had our R1 rifles. We jumped into an abandoned Swapo trench and tried to figure out where all the shooting was coming from. But then we decided the trench was the wrong place to be and we started running again. How far I don't know, we just wanted to get away from all that enemy fire.'

The next moment, dead ahead, he saw three bright flashes from the muzzle of a rifle. 'One bullet tore a gouge out of my knee but I froze, I just stood there, I froze. But old Van shoved me to the ground and shot the terr who had just shot me.'

They crawled behind a large anthill, 'but they saw us and one of those 14,5 mil machine guns opened up on us.'

Bullets thudded into the anthill and showered them with leaves and twigs. Tears started to run down their smoke-blackened faces,

Marco remembers, 'and then Van said: "Marco, we are going to die here."'

Somehow those words made the Italian boy from Joburg dig deeper. 'I said no, we are not dying here, my man. Today we won't die. I remember it well because he was one of the few Afrikaans guys in our section. So he was talking Afrikaans and I was answering in English.'

All that training started to kick in. Like firing single shots instead of bursts, and then only when you have a clear target, in order to save ammo. This was no time for 'spray and pray' like you saw in those Vietnam movies: 'I only had one full magazine [20 rounds]. You could see the terrs running through the bush in groups of three and they clearly knew where we were.'

And Marco had a new problem: ants attracted by the fresh blood from his wounds crawled into his browns. Soon he was cursing at their stinging bites. But bullets were still whacking clods of clay-like earth off the anthill and they had no choice but to stay put.

'I kept telling Van only to shoot when he can see what he's shooting at. And eventually he said: "Oukei, Caforio, oukei."'

PAUL LOUW

Back in Bloemfontein, Colonel 'Oom Ep' van Lill used to ask his students the same question over and over: 'When do you know you've won the war?'

The answer, straight from Sun Tzu's *The Art of War*, was imprinted on Paul's memory: when you alone remain standing on the battlefield.

It was with that philosophy in mind that he set out, alone and unarmed, to find his Bravo section, which to the best of his knowledge had not come to grief. He wanted to rally them and the survivors of the other sections and continue the fight.

When Paul and the others start recalling those moments of blood and chaos, they automatically revert to the lingo of boys on a battlefield. Section 2 becomes 'Bravo' and section 3 'Charlie'.

The burned flesh of his arm was hurting, but he was unaware that he also had shrapnel in his leg. On his way to where he thought Bravo section was, another Ratel stopped beside him. It was Lieutenant Chris de Klerk, commander of Platoon 2. Contrary to Harmse's order to 'stand fast', Chris had moved his own platoon up to assist Paul and his men.

'I said to him: "Chris, just give me a rifle." And he said wryly: "Why are you running around the bush by yourself? Go back to your troops, they need you." So I told him to carry on, I had to go find my Bravo section, and I ran around his Ratel and into the bush.'

Suddenly he found himself looking into the barrel of Corporal Gary Braithwaite's rifle. [Gary was Bravo's section leader.] 'I threw my hands in the air and shouted: "Don't shoot! Stop, stop, stop!"'

'I told him to hand me his tail gunner's rifle and that we were going to take his section back to my Ratel and then fight on foot through this enemy base, a real fire-and-move section assault.'

Just like he had trained so hard to do under the critical eye of Oom Ep in Bloemfontein and Dippenaar at Omuthiya.

GARETH RUTHERFORD

Gareth and his Bravo section buddies were in defensive positions outside Ratel 21B when they saw Paul running towards them across the battlefield.

'You would think our loot was armour-plated. He was burned and his face was blackened by smoke … He talked frantically to

Braithwaite but I could not hear what was said as we were firing at every little bush. But then Gary relayed the order: "We have to go clear the trenches."'

Their situation was dire. 'We had nowhere to go, for the enemy was in front and on our flanks and Platoon 2 was moving up from behind. It was terrifying, but amid all that chaos Paul pulled us together.'

They started to fight their way back, textbook style, and came across a 23 mil protected by a sand berm and some Swapo troops in a trench: 'Three of them started to jog away at a leisurely pace, grinning as if they had no cares in the world. Vossie, our gunner, opened up with the Browning and McLean fired his big Bren machine gun from the hip … the Swapos were literally blown to pieces. I chucked two grenades at the emplacement and provided covering fire for the other guys.'

Then, as they got closer to Ratel 21C (the borrowed 9G), Gareth started hearing the frantic cries of 'Medic, medic!' And that meant him.

With the 23 mil out of action, he ran over to the stricken vehicle: 'It was crazy, surreal … I saw a dead body lying next to the vehicle, but the engine was still running.'

He crawled through the door and found himself in a slaughter-house. The 23 mil rounds had penetrated from the front and a hand grenade had detonated inside, he would later hear.

'There was another dead body on the Ratel floor and blood dripped from the turret. I crawled through all the broken glass and blood to reach the dead man's stop [the cut switch for the engine in case the driver was killed instantly], but it would not work. The air pressure tank was holed and it made a terrific hissing noise.

'It seemed like everybody was dead. Corporal Paul Kruger [the

Springbok gymkhana rider]. Steve Cronjé, the driver. Mike, my running mate from high school days … On top of the Ratel was the lifeless Frank Lello and on the ground lay Rob de Vito's upper body.'

Gareth shouted for somebody to bring his big medical bag, which was still in his own Ratel, 21B. Jan Hoevers drove over and Vos, the gunner, handed Gareth the bag.

He soon realised not everybody inside was dead. Peter Warrener's leg was virtually torn off but he was alive. So was Martin French, his body full of shrapnel, and Andrew Madden. 'I felt overwhelmed, but realised I was the only one who could help them and I stared doing what I was trained to do.

'Andrew had lost a lot of blood and I struggled to insert the needles for the drip bags, because trauma caused the arteries to collapse. I amputated Peter's leg and tied it off with field dressings … I dressed everybody's wounds as best I could, gave them Sustagen and prepared them for the casevac.'

PAUL LOUW

When Paul ran off into the bush to find the men of Bravo section, he did not see HP fall. But now, while fighting back to his own Ratel, he discovered his badly wounded driver lying on the ground.

So many years after that day he still finds it incredible that HP could survive a direct hit by the same weapon that punched through armour with such devastating force. How was it possible?

'And maybe it was the work of a higher hand, I don't know, but just then a Ratel came racing up behind us and it was one of the ambulance Ratels.'

He signalled for the vehicle to stop, and as it slowed down the hydraulic door swung open. What he saw hit him like a gut punch: 'There were all these wounded guys inside. Where they all came from, I had no idea. One of the doctors who accompanied us, a thin guy with a moustache, was sitting by the left-hand door with tears streaming down his face. He kept shouting, "Close the door, close the door!" Braithwaite and I basically hurled HP into the Ratel and the door closed and they raced off again.'

They continued doing fire-and-movement until they reached Paul's still-blazing vehicle. 'But all kinds of munitions were going off inside, there was nothing to be done.'

For the first time since the fighting started, he started to fully grasp what a severe price his platoon was paying. The dead in his own Ratel 21 were his signaller, Steve Loubser, his platoon medic, Piet Joubert, and Vaatjie Venter, who did not even need to be there.

'Vaatjie was actually the storeman back at Omuthiya, but he came to me and said there was no way he was going to be left behind. So I made him my tail gunner and gave him a crash course on operating the Browning. How to fire it, how to clear stoppages, all of that. Anyway, when we got back to the Ratel, I realised there was nothing to be done for those three guys. They were incinerated.'

He was grateful that he and Braithwaite could get HP into the ambulance Ratel, but he had no way of knowing whether he would live.

From his own vehicle, they went to Ratel 21A and found that Gertjie Kemp was still clinging to life in his driver's seat. Bravo section again took up defensive positions while Kemp was carefully lifted out. But he was not the only victim they found.

'When we got there, I saw Fourietjie [JH Fourie, the backup driver of Ratel 21A] apparently just sitting on top of the Ratel while there was heavy enemy fire coming from the bush all around us. I lost my temper and pulled him by his boot, shouting, "Come down from up there!"'

Paul did not know that Fourie was already dead. 'And then he fell over on top of me. They'd shot him in the stomach and his blood and intestines poured over me.'

For a moment Paul lost his mind: 'I just stood there banging my fist against the Ratel asking: "Why is this happening? Why is it happening to me? If it's like this over here, what is happening at the other objectives? How are we going to get out of here? Do we have to walk back to South West Africa?"'

Tears streaked the soot on his face but he pulled himself together and once again organised the surviving troops – including the slightly wounded – in a defensive circle around 21A: 'You guys cover the area from that tree to the next one, and you guys over here shoot anything that moves from there to there …'

But the troops from Charlie section were still missing in action: 'And I realised, okay, we have to get to 21C … I could see it over there and smoke was billowing from it and it did not look good.'

Ratel 21C was about 100 m from their present position. In thick bush, surrounded by enemy and with bullets still flying, that was a hell of a distance. But once again, with Braithwaite's help, Paul lined the guys up and they started doing fire-and-movement towards 21C. (In fire-and-movement, every second man provides covering fire while the guys flanking him advance, then they switch, and so on.)

Fortunately, Swapo's heavy hitters, the 23s and 14,5s, had already been taken out.

'We drew fire from Swapo fighters a few times but we took them out and kept advancing. One was a sharpshooter up a tree. But nothing too hectic.'

And then they reached Ratel 21C. The first shock was seeing the two halves of De Vito's body. Next was Andrew Madden, lying on his face next to the Ratel. 'When we pulled up his shirt his entire back was full of shrapnel ... I knew he was not going to make it.'

The section leader, Paul Kruger, was dead in his turret. 'We had to cut him loose because the 23 mil round went through his chest. Their driver, Cronjé, was also in his seat, ripped to shreds by shrapnel.'

Paul has only the utmost respect for Gareth: 'Under extreme pressure and working alone, he got all the wounded together, prioritised the most serious cases, and did what he could to comfort and save them ... like he was trained to do.'

MARCO CAFORIO

Behind the anthill where he and Van were sheltering, Marco suddenly heard the roar of Ratel engines, 'maybe the length of a soccer field away but getting closer'.

It was Platoon 3, but he did not know and cared even less. They were friendly – nothing else mattered. He saw that the bush in that direction was not as dense. 'I said to Van, "I hear Ratels, let's go," and he said "no". I said, "Van, if we stay here, we are going to die."'

As he rose, Marco could feel the shrapnel cutting deeper into his leg and a fresh gush of warm blood: 'But you hop and skip and do whatever you have to, because your brain tells you that you have to keep moving. Then I saw them: one, two, three, four Ratels. One of them stopped and the 20 mil barrel swung towards us and I thought, hell, are they going to shoot us after all this?'

But the gunner – 'George Vermaak, he lives in Cape Town now' – started firing at the 14,5 mil that had them pinned down

The wounded Marco Caforio (just visible on the far right) with his arm around a buddy's shoulders.

behind the anthill for so long. 'And then, as we were running towards the Ratel, I was hit in my back and ankle and at the same time I heard Van say that he was also wounded. I asked "Where?" because I did not want to turn and look.

'For a while I just lay there on the ground and then I felt somebody lift me up and it was old Kelvin, Kelvin Luke from Platoon 3, and he was yelling, "Come on, Caforio, get up!" He dragged me to his Ratel, but I was so buggered by now, all I could think of was that it hurt even more.'

Kelvin saved his life, he stresses: 'I would be dead if he hadn't left the safety of his Ratel to come and get me.'

When they got there, Van was already being helped inside. But Marco, with the horror inside his own Ratel still fresh in his mind, dug in his heels. Eventually they had to force him inside: 'I sat in the back and all I was worried about was to check how much ammo I had left. I counted three bullets in my magazine and the next moment that damn 14,5 that had us pinned down hit the Ratel, punching straight through the door.

'I think what saved Kelvin's life was the huge metal towbar mounted on the outside of the hull. I think it absorbed the worst of the 14,5 hits, but he was wounded nevertheless. And I was hit by shrapnel again, this time in my face.'

His face and eye burned like fire and everything was getting darker: 'But I did not want to pass out, because I believed I would die if I did. I started to scream: "I don't want to die, I don't want to die!" A lance corporal, I think it was Vermaak, slapped me and said: "You are not going to die."'

A medic shoved pills in his hand and said: 'Swallow these.' Marco saw they were covered in his own blood and worried how he was going to get them down. But he did, and as a field dressing was wrapped around his head the powerful medication kicked in and he started drifting in and out of consciousness.

He remembers being transferred to an ambulance Ratel and seeing HP inside. 'I called his name and he said: "Marco, they got me, they got me." Then I passed out. There were other wounded guys but I don't know who. My brain was not working.'

He was vaguely aware of artillery shells falling close by (harassment fire on Dippenaar's orders, to keep Swapo's heads down). 'And I thought, okay, if they hit me now, if I die, that's cool. When you get high on those pills you stop caring.'

The only thing that mattered was that the pain, stress and anxiety were gone for now.

'Then we got to the casevac area. HP was the first to be airlifted.

A panoramic view of Smokeshell shows a Puma helicopter evacuating casualties.

One of the wounded at Smokeshell receives attention.

I remember they thought he was already gone, dead. I was less severely wounded than some of the other guys, so I sat with my back against a tree and waited for my turn.'

He sat there while three or four other guys were airlifted. 'I think the sun was starting to go down when I tried to get up but couldn't move and just started shouting: "Put me in the fucking chopper!"'

Much later, Kelvin Luke told him the chopper could not land at first because one of the Swapo anti-aircraft guns was firing at it. But finally Marco was in the belly of the Puma and he felt it rise and turn sharply to the south. 'Kelvin told me even then those green tracers were streaking past the chopper ... I never even realised they were shooting at us.'

He remembers how the setting sun seemed like a bloodied eye peering through a haze of smoke above the bush: 'I thought, jeez, I made it, I'm saved. Then I cracked and started calling for Rob de Vito in case he was among the other wounded in the chopper. I threw up, maybe from all the adrenaline, and they shoved more drip needles into me.'

Still in Angola, the chopper landed at a forward medical post, 'I think about 20 klicks away and there were doctors. They asked where I was wounded, cut my boots and browns away and examined me. Then I heard, "Okay, he can go," and I was casevaced across the border to Oshakati. We got there after dark.'

The first thing he saw at Oshakati was two body bags, 'and I cracked up again, because I was alive. While I was being X-rayed there was more vomiting and the technicians just kept telling me: "Don't worry about it, it's okay."'

The rest of that night he was only sporadically aware of his surroundings. At long last he was on an operating table, and a surgeon – 'I remember he had a red beard and an American accent' – looked at his X-ray plates and said: 'Son, you're lucky to be alive.'

Marco turned his head to a clock on the wall, saw it was 23h30 and sank into oblivion.

GARETH RUTHERFORD

The young medic felt deeply alone in the hell that was Charlie section's Ratel. Around Gareth, the guys who had trained and suffered and laughed with him were dead or wounded. He laboured to save their lives while praying to hear the sound of approaching choppers.

Section medics were not doctors or surgeons. They were regular infantry soldiers who, after the day's combat drills, received extra training in how to stabilise wounded buddies on the battlefield until they could be casevaced to a medical post or clinic.

Today, any civilian paramedic will tell you about the golden hour – that crucial window of time to get a badly injured person from, say, an accident scene to an operating theatre. Get him to a surgeon in under an hour and you boost his chances of survival. If not, the clock starts working against you.

'There was Mike, my school running mate. And Gert Kemp. Some guys say he died in his driver's seat, but he did not. Years later I told Kempie's brother that he died under my hands.

'I tied off wounds to stop the bleeding, cleaned and bandaged them, even amputated a leg. Gave them Sustagen and did everything to stabilise and ready them for the casevac.'

'Everybody was doing okay. I asked Peter Warrener, whose leg I removed, how he was feeling and he said: "Fine." I spoke to Nick Ogilvy, who was full of shrapnel, and tried to remove his shirt.

But he said: "No, Gareth, help the others first." They were all so brave while they lay there bleeding. Their only concern was for their friends and brothers, not for themselves.'

Peter was lying in the sun next to the Ratel and Gareth gingerly moved him into the shade of a tree: 'I was afraid moving him would hurt. I asked him if he had any pain but he said: "No, nothing." And then he just went to sleep. Gone, for ever. It was a hell of a shock for me.'

Andrew Madden had a gaping wound in his neck. 'I tried to close it, I tried everything. I believe that as a medic I did all the right things.'

He battled to insert the drip needles into veins that had collapsed due to trauma and shock: 'Andrew begged me to get the drip in. As I pushed needle after needle into him, he said: "It's starting to get dark now."

'They all said, "Please Gareth, we don't want to die." But time was not on their side.'

Gareth held their hands and prayed with them. They all remained hopeful, he recalls.

After Paul Louw and the survivors he had rallied cleared the immediate vicinity of the enemy, they carried Gert Kemp over to where Gareth was caring for the other wounded in the lee of Charlie section's destroyed Ratel: 'He had shrapnel in his chest and one eye. I turned him on his side so the blood could run out of his lungs. It was such a relief when he regained consciousness.'

But the golden hour had long since passed: 'They kept telling me the choppers were on their way ... A senior officer arrived to see what the situation was and I shouted at him: "It's been two hours and still no choppers!" He said they were coming, but I was so angry.'

When help arrived it was in the shape of Rifleman Peter Brent.

'I was so grateful to Peter. He helped to comfort the guys and kept them calm. And I was so grateful not to be alone anymore.'

Brent was a friend of Andrew Madden's and also battled to get drip needles into his collapsed veins. Like Gareth, he held the hands of the wounded, read to them from a pocket Bible and prayed with them.

Finally, a Ratel arrived to take the wounded to where a rough landing zone had been prepared, but the choppers came too late for Andrew Madden. As he drew his last breath, Peter Brent held his hand and read words of comfort from the Bible.

One of the wounded not under his care, Gareth recalls, was unintentionally left behind. Piet Joubert, the platoon medic, was presumed dead after being hit by small arms fire while exiting Paul Louw's burning Ratel. But the next day his body was discovered in a sitting position in a deserted Swapo trench. Exactly when he succumbed to his wounds, nobody knows.

JAN HOEVERS

The former assistant train driver who waived his exemption from military service in order to get on in life now found himself in an unfamiliar situation.

You don't often see a Ratel driver footslogging on the battlefield – especially if his vehicle is still in good working order. But Paul needed every available man.

'I fell in with the other survivors and we started clearing trenches ... I was on foot with my R1 rifle,' he says, as if he still can't quite believe it.

Like most of the young troopies who survived that traumatic day, his memories are somewhat jumbled. At some stage the cavalry arrived – Captain Jab Swart and a force dispatched by Dippenaar. Jab's orders were to collect the living, the wounded, the dead and the destroyed Ratels. Having done so, he was to lead them to a rear area where the battle group would go into a defensive laager for the night.

But first there was more drama for Jan. He recalls a 'vaguely familiar senior officer' ordering him and his friend Willem (a fellow member of Bravo section) to collect the weapons and ID documents of the Swapo dead.

'As we were moving around, they started shooting at us. So we ran to a slit trench cleared earlier and I dived in first and I heard Willem say, "but there's no room for both of us". But I just grabbed him and pulled him in on top of me, because they were still shooting.'

They had a brief conversation and agreed they could not stay in their crowded shelter for too long: 'So Willem leaped out and started running and I followed and as we ran you could hear the bullets going "phew phew phew" past your ears. We were so flipping scared, we ran crouched over so low that our knees were up past our ears.'

They were still running for safety when Jan suddenly saw his Ratel start up and move away. Unbeknown to him, the dead and wounded had been transferred to his vehicle while he was wandering about rifling the pockets of enemy corpses. Behind the wheel was Gareth Rutherford.

'Then I really started running! When I got to the Ratel I banged on the hull with my rifle barrel. Gareth stopped and told me to get in. But I said: "No, that's my seat, *you* get out."'

Back in his rightful place, Jan fell in with the convoy withdrawing from the Swapo positions. It was no picnic, he recalls. Ratel 21B was overcrowded, the wounded were in pain and the convoy was still drawing enemy fire. 'At one stage the Ratel ahead of me fell into a trench or bunker and I had to wait while they got it out; it took a long time.'

Needless to say, any stationary Ratel was a tempting target: 'I saw one RPG rocket flashing past in front of us and another one flew overhead. And when I could finally drive off, another one went behind us.'

Jan saw the Swapo soldier who was firing at them, 'and I shouted at Vos, our gunner: "There he is, left, left!" Vos swung the turret around to get him with the 20 mil but the barrel kept smacking against a stout tree branch ... finally the branch snapped, but by now the barrel was bent so he shot the terr with the Browning instead.'

Finally, he could stop at the chopper landing zone to unload the wounded, then it was onwards to the overnight laager. By this time darkness had fallen, and he strained his eyes to keep the tiny red navigation light of the Ratel ahead of him in sight as they churned over and around trees.

At last, he could stop and switch off for the night: 'As we climbed out of the Ratels everyone immediately started asking who made it alive. As the dead were named, I counted them off on my fingers one by one ... and 12 of our 44 did not make it.'

The other guys unrolled their brown sleeping bags on the ground but Jan clambered back into his crowded driver's compartment: 'I was dead tired. It was stifling hot and I think the adrenaline makes you sweat even more, because I was sitting in a puddle of sweat on my seat. I remember gulping down about two litres of water and then I just fell into the deepest sleep imaginable.'

But Paul Louw, who was only two Ratels behind Jan's when RPGs started flying at the tail of the convoy, was far less fortunate.

PAUL LOUW

As platoon commander, Paul felt responsible for the wounded 'but Gareth took the medical situation out of my hands'.

So he left Gareth at 21C to do the best he could, led his handful of troops back to Ratel 21A and once again took up a defensive position: 'It was in a bit of a fold in the ground, so that gave us some natural protection, and we had a fairly good view over the whole area.'

Elsewhere on the sprawling Swapo base complex, combat teams 2 and 3 were attacking their own designated targets, but Paul still had no idea of what the bigger picture looked like. His world was confined to what he could see, hear and feel in this spot where those damned anti-aircraft guns had shredded his platoon. So many of his troops were dead or wounded and the surrounding bush was still crawling with enemy soldiers … he badly needed help.

When he bailed out of his burning Ratel, he grabbed his manpack radio (the lightweight radios carried by infantry soldiers on their backs), for the vehicle-mounted radios were knocked out. 'Then I called "Zero" [Dippenaar's call sign] on the designated channel, but there was no response. Then I called "all stations" over and over, every ten minutes. But nobody answered. Finally I just said: "All stations, this is 21," and explained my situation in case anybody was listening … So many dead, so many wounded, I need support. Can anybody help?'

And finally a voice came from the telephone-like radio handset. It belonged to Koos van Rensburg, a high school friend attached to the anti-tank element. 'And Koos said: "Paul, if nobody else wants to go and get you, I will."'

But as Paul was about to rejoice another voice cut in – that of his company commander, Louis Harmse. And he heard Harmse say: 'Koos van Rensburg, if you go in there [where Paul was] I will court martial you.'

And that was the end of that.

What Paul did not know at that moment was that Dippenaar had already replaced Harmse with Jab Swart and duly ordered the latter: 'Go and get Paul. Get him and his guys together, see what's going on and salvage what you can.'

And finally Jab arrived at their position with a force of four Ratels: 'With Jab came Kobus Moolman, an anti-tank guy who was on the mech course with me. And André van Tonder, whose sister I would one day marry.'

Paul and his troops were overjoyed to see Jab and his four Ratels. But Paul's long day was about to turn into an even longer night.

8
A NIGHT ON THE KILLING FIELD

In the film *Fury*, an American tank crew is left stranded in German-held territory after detonating a landmine. They're soon engulfed in a night-long battle with SS troops trying to storm their immobilised Sherman tank. The Hollywood movie hit the big screens 34 years after Smokeshell, but Paul Louw and his comrades would surely identify with parts of it.

Paul picks up where Jab Swart led his four Ratels up to their defensive position: 'I got into Kobus Moolman's Ratel 90 and we loaded some of the dead and wounded. But just then Swapo started attacking us from the north … The light was fading; we could still see, but not too well. They poured a lot of small arms fire at us and we could see the bright flashes of RPGs coming at us.'

They departed with some haste, but now they were the last Ratel in the convoy as it withdrew from the Swapo position: 'And then the big engine block of Kobus's Ratel [at the rear of the vehicle] was hit by an RPG. We managed to keep moving for another 150 m or so before we shuddered to a halt. But the other vehicles ahead just kept going … and there we were, stranded on the objective and now it's getting really dark.'

Paul would later learn that Dippenaar was furious when he heard that Moolman's stricken Ratel had been left behind. But first, a long night in the midst of the enemy lay ahead.

Inside the Ratel, it was pretty cramped. (A Ratel 90 had the same hull as the infantry derivative, but it was married to the turret and 90 mm cannon of the Eland armoured car. Some of the interior space was taken up by racks for the big 90 mm shells.)

The Ratel 90 had a crew of four or five, 'and then there was the wounded Chris Raats and me. And we had two deceased in there with us as well,' Paul explains.

'In the turret Kobus is swearing black and blue because nothing is working. The engine is dead, the radio battery is almost flat, nobody is answering our calls and the enemy is out there.'

The rattle of small arms had fallen silent 'because they probably could not see us, at least initially. Kobus asked what we should do and I said: "We're safest inside the Ratel, unless they walk right up to us and hit us with an RPG."

'But I just knew Swapo would not have the guts to come too close. So we made turns to stand sentry in the turret, looking and listening for any approaching enemy. The rest of us were to stay inside, as quiet as possible, until dawn.'

It was a hellish night. There was no room to stretch out cramping limbs and the wounded Chris Raats moaned in agony. Worst of all was trying to imagine what was happening in the inky blackness outside. Where is the enemy? What are they up to? Are they sneaking up on us?

To make matters worse, the artillery kept up a constant barrage in order to give Swapo a sleepless night: 'So all night long we're sitting there in the dark while our own artillery shells are coming in. It was a terrifying experience for all of us.'

Finally, Kobus spoke up: 'Paul, find my Infantry School weekend bag, it's down there somewhere.'

Paul had to grope around for the bag in the dark. Made from soft imitation leather, it was easy to identify by touch – just about everything else was made of rough canvas or metal. When he got it, Kobus instructed him: 'There's a bottle of brandy inside, get it out.'

Kobus had been a naval officer, Paul remembers with a touch of humour, and he clearly kept the traditions of the high seas alive in the bush – no matter that it was brandy and not rum.

'So we passed that bottle around all night, one sip at a time. I also gave some to Chris Raats to try and quiet him down a bit. Now, alcohol makes a wound bleed faster, but we had him patched up pretty good. So we felt confident he would not bleed out too much.'

And the brandy was all they had left to give him, for all the other medication was used up.

They had not managed to raise anybody on the vehicle radio before the battery died, 'so we had no idea whether anybody was going to come and get us or not'.

Throughout that endless night, the sentries in the turret could see the fires of Swapo encampments in the surrounding bush, 200 to 300 m away. They could hear enemy soldiers calling to each other, their voices amplified by the night. And worst of all, they seemed to be aware of the stranded Ratel. For every once in a while, a distant figure walked a bit closer and then the velvety darkness was torn by the flash and roar of a rocket.

Just pot shots, Paul recalls, nothing very accurate. He still suspects they did not have the guts to come too close in the dark.

'How many times it happened I can't say. You heard the guy in the turret say: "Here it comes, here it comes … and he missed!" So it went all night. Maybe four, five, seven times? I never counted.'

What mattered was that none of the RPG hollow-charge

warheads hit the Ratel. But Paul was convinced: 'As soon as the sun was up, they would come for us.'

So, well before dawn, every man took as much spare ammunition, water and rations as they could carry. Quietly they emerged from the Ratel, careful to avoid the clanging sound of metal against metal. Paul took the Browning machine gun off its mount and hefted it onto his shoulder, one of the ammo belts looped around his body.

And they started to walk off in search of their own forces. For if the sun found them here, they would surely die.

JAN HOEVERS

Paul and his 'lost patrol' were already hoofing it when Jan awoke from a bottomless sleep in his driver's seat. But he felt anything but upbeat and refreshed.

'As the guys clambered out of their sleeping bags and vehicles, they all seemed in a kind of daze. We sat around on top of the Ratels and talked about what happened to us. We were dirty and drained.'

By this time they had a better picture of the terrible losses Platoon 1 had suffered the previous day. Their lieutenant, Paul Louw, was missing and three other guys in his Ratel 21 were dead. Section 2 had suffered two dead. The blood price paid by section 3 was unimaginable – seven dead. And their company second-in-command, Lieutenant Hannes du Toit, was dead.

Their mates through all the afkak and laughs of the past 18 months – gone forever. Whether Marco, HP and the other wounded borne away on choppers would survive, they could only guess.

For Jan, it was surreal to think that only he remained of Platoon 1's four Ratel drivers. How does something like that happen?

Just a few metres from his Ratel was a square tent. The night before, as the adrenaline and stress of the day drained away, he took scant notice of it. But now he watched in horror as body bags were carried out of the tent: 'Those were our guys in the bags. It was just heartbreaking. Just the previous morning we were all alive, now a third of us were zipped up in those bags.'

His section was asked if they felt up to returning to the battle zone to help recover two of their platoon Ratels (Paul's and 21C). They discussed it among themselves first, Jan recalls. It was a miracle that they were the only section to come through the fight unharmed, they told each other – even when so many RPGs were launched at them. The tragedy would have been even greater if they had also copped it.

Jan was one of those who chose not to go back: 'So we just hung around while the others went to assist with the recovery.'

Later, he regretted his choice: 'But at that stage you're so scared. I never knew one could be that scared. When I was running and heard those bullets whizzing past me, I realised that life hangs on a very, very thin thread. I was so terrified. I remember one corporal said he was so scared he could hardly get upright. He wanted to walk but his legs refused to carry him.'

Smokeshell taught him to pray. 'You know, eventually I could recite the words of Psalm 23, about "wandering through the valley of the shadow of death", in my sleep.'

PAUL LOUW

Navigation was a simple matter. When the Ratel gave up the ghost its nose was still pointing in the direction the other Ratels were going.

Their plan was to head off in the same direction and follow the wheel tracks of the convoy until they got to somebody who did not greet them with rifle fire. They agreed it would be safer to walk inside the tyre tracks because any landmines would already have been detonated by a big Ratel wheel. Of course they could walk into an ambush, but they would just have to deal with that if and when it happened.

It was no easy trek. Chris Raats could not walk because his legs were full of shrapnel. They had no stretcher so they took turns to carry him piggyback style or using the 'skaapdra' technique: draped over both shoulders, like they did during basic training until their legs buckled.

It was slow going. There was the ever-present danger of walking into the enemy, or that Chris could utter a cry of pain at just the wrong moment. With every step they expected to draw fire, but thankfully the bush remained quiet.

The sun grew hotter and the soft sand sucked at their boots. Even big, strong Paul felt his strength starting to ebb. The Browning was a bugger to carry, for even without a tripod and belt of ammunition it weighed 14 kg. It was a chunk of deadweight with sharp edges that bit into your hands and dragged at your shoulders.

He started to realise they were not going to make it if they had to keep carrying Chris: 'We could not move fast enough to cover any meaningful distance. And what happens if we walk into a contact [firefight] while carrying him?'

You never leave a buddy behind. That was the military code they lived by. No matter what. But the going got harder and harder.

Then he heard the sweet hum of helicopter rotors. He looked up and saw a flight of Alouette gunships, those beautiful dragonflies with deadly stings.

Paul was also humping his manpack radio, even though he knew the battery was exhausted. But somehow, when he pressed in the contact plate on the handset and called the choppers on their channel, he got an immediate reply: 'I said: "We are right beneath you, we have a wounded guy and you have to take him off our hands because we can't carry him anymore."'

Negative, came the answer. We are gunships, we don't have room for wounded and it's dangerous to land here.

'And I said: "I don't care what you do, you can protect each other, but somebody has to land."'

He may or may not have threatened to shoot at them with the Browning. Whatever the case, this time they replied with a 'Roger, pop some smoke.'

Alouette helicopters were indeed much smaller than the workhorse Pumas. The latter could ferry a section of parabats or a number of wounded, but the Alouette could accommodate little more than its crew of three and the 20 mm cannon mounted in the side door.

'We basically tied Chris onto the top of that gun in a spreadeagled position. Then the chopper lifted off and we started walking again.'

Finally, they came across the north–south dirt road that Paul had used as a reference point on his way to attack the target the previous day. They had walked 25 to 30 km but were still in Swapo's backyard.

'So I said to Kobus, let's set up an ambush along the road, capture the first Swapo vehicle that comes along and then we use that to carry on looking for our own forces. We just had to be careful to not destroy the vehicle when we took out the enemy soldiers.'

So Paul, being the infantry officer (Kobus was anti-tank), showed the guys their positions and fields of fire. Wait for me to

Corporal Paul Kruger, the gymkhana rider, was the first to die.

The gravestone of Peter 'Pip' Warrener.

fire the first shot, he told them, and then just take everybody out. And lo and behold, they heard a vehicle approaching. But no fireworks were necessary, for it was one of their own – a lone Buffel troop carrier. Apart from the driver it was empty. 'So I waved him down and asked where he was going and he said, "To the echelon" and I said, "Okay, we're going with you."'

When they reached the echelon, they were taken straight to Dippenaar's cluster of command Ratels: 'There was great surprise when we jumped from the Buffel because everyone believed we were dead, killed the previous night – and here we were in the flesh.'

There was not much time to congratulate himself, however, because a heart-wrenching task awaited him. One by one, he unzipped the body bags of his dead troops to identify them and collect their dog tags (stainless steel identification discs).

Then he recorded their names in his report, all 12 of them.

From his own Ratel 21: riflemen FJ (Steve) Loubser, Piet Joubert and CJ (Vaatjie) Venter. KIA (killed in action).

From section 1 (Ratel 21A): riflemen Gertjie Kemp (driver) and JH Fourie (backup driver). KIA.

From section 3 (Ratel 21C): Corporal Paul Kruger (section leader) and riflemen Steve Cronjé (driver), Peter Warrener, Frank Lello, MC Luyt, Robert de Vito and Andrew Madden. KIA.

His platoon's 17 wounded, including HP and Marco, had already been flown out to Grootfontein and beyond.

'I was also wounded but I did not want to leave. The shrapnel in my calf and the burn wounds on my arm did not really bug me. I just think, given the circumstances, I preferred to ignore it.'

For there was still a lot to do and the challenges for Dippenaar and his command group were huge. The sprawling Smokeshell complex had to be cleared, trench by trench and bunker by bunker.

That meant that all remaining enemy troops had to be flushed out and killed or captured; all useful enemy vehicles, armaments and munitions had to be loaded and hauled back across the border; and all possible documents and other intelligence had to collected for analysis by the experts in Pretoria.

All damaged or destroyed 61 Mech vehicles had to be recovered from the battlefield, because you leave nothing behind for your enemy to gloat over or glean information from. And then there was the enormous task of refuelling, rearming and feeding the entire combat group in the Angolan bush in order to get them battle- and march-ready.

Dippenaar and his crew did not emerge entirely unscathed from this fluid battlefield with no fixed front lines. On day one of the attack, anti-aircraft fire narrowly missed Dippenaar in his turret. And on day two, while following close on the heels of the fighting sections sweeping through enemy positions, his Ratel detonated what appeared to be a double 'cheese mine' (two vehicle mines linked for a more powerful blast).

Thankfully, nobody was injured, but eyewitnesses related how General Constand Viljoen, Chief of the Army, shot out of his hatch 'like a cork from a bottle' and hit the ground on his feet. A bemused Dippenaar had to look on while his crippled Ratel was towed away by the tiffies.

While Dippenaar got on with the bigger picture in his usual calm and controlled manner, Paul paid close attention to the welfare of the remaining troops in his platoon: 'There were only 12 of them left and everybody was in a state of shock.' Leaving them behind was the last thing on his mind. And it never occurred to him that he might not be all that emotionally healthy after all he had seen and endured.

Many of the troops noticed an 'elderly, unfamiliar officer with a strange-looking rifle' who sporadically popped up where they were working or brewing a quick firebucket of ratpack coffee. Few of them recognised General Viljoen. The 'funny rifle' dangling from his shoulder was a prototype R4, cloned from Israel's Galil assault rifle and soon to replace the R1 as the army's frontline weapon.

It was the general himself who sat down with Paul for a quiet chat. His fit troops were going to be assigned to other platoons, which could make the absence of their dead buddies less painful, he heard: 'And then he told me it would mean a lot more for my wounded troops to have me with them.'

But Paul had one more thing to do. While checking a bunker after the big battle he had found some newborn puppies and caught one: 'The eyes were not even fully open yet. I gave the puppy to somebody in a Ratel and said, "Look after him and take him back to Omuthiya."'

At that moment Paul had no idea of the role this four-legged war orphan was destined to play in his life.

Then, on D-day plus two, he grudgingly climbed into a chopper that took him away from Smokeshell, with its trenches filled with the dead, twisted metal and the stench of fires fuelled by rubber, cordite, diesel and flesh.

PART 2

BEYOND
SMOKESHELL

9

HP AND PHIA

In the homes of many Smokeshell veterans, you'll find a special corner where they commemorate the devastating day that changed their young lives for ever. You'll see, among other things, yellowed newspaper clippings recording the faces and names of their fallen brothers-in-arms, the 61 Mech badge they once wore on their sun-bleached uniform sleeves, and the motivational card distributed by Dippenaar on the morning of the assault.

And there is always that iconic Border War photograph with Ratels in the foreground and plumes of black smoke rising above the bush. In the centre, a Puma helicopter lifts off the ground, nose down and tail up to gather speed. On board was the severely injured HP Ferreira.

The image was the work of Willem Steenkamp, at the time a *Cape Times* journalist who had been called up, in his capacity as a Citizen Force (reserve) officer, to accompany Dippenaar's combat group and record the assault on Smokeshell.

But in the Bloemfontein home of HP and his wife, Phia, pride of place goes to another picture taken just moments earlier. It shows the 'deceased' HP on a stretcher as he is rushed to that same helicopter. 'There,' says HP as he points to his younger self

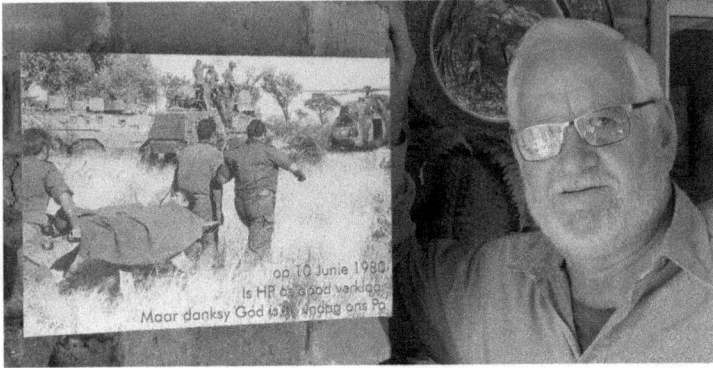

Hennie 'HP' Ferreira with the picture showing him being stretchered to a Puma helicopter.

in the posterised image on his living room wall, 'you can see I'm lifting my head, I'm alive.'

When the picture was originally released to the media, his face was blacked out by the pen of a vigilant army censor because HP had been reported as dead. The error caused a bit of a furore and it's not quite clear how it happened. But, figuratively speaking, HP rose from the dead like Lazarus and that's all that really matters.

He remembers little of the chopper flight to Oshakati, the nearest base south of the border with an adequate medical facility: 'I could not feel my lower body. It was just gone, and the rest of me was shaking badly.'

At Oshakati, overworked surgeons in bloodstained theatre scrubs did what they could before he was airlifted to the military hospital at Grootfontein and from there to Pretoria.

HP was oblivious to it all: 'I was in a coma for seven days. My first real memory is of seeing my father's face next to my bed in Pretoria. And he said: "Son, do you remember your parting words when I dropped you off at the filling station outside Theunissen that day?

You said you'll come home again ... but you won't be whole."'

HP had plenty of time to reflect on the prophetic nature of those words as surgeons stitched him back together again. Bit by bit, one operation at a time. For the next three years, 1 Military Hospital (1 Mil) in Voortrekkerhoogte would be HP's home.

The comments and updates of the medical staff on his bed chart made interesting reading, HP remembers wryly. The big 14,5 mm round had torn up his insides: 'The doctors did not think I was going to make it; there was just too much damage. Two-thirds of my colon and small intestine was gone, so was my bladder and kidney tubes. My coccyx bone was smashed and one hip torn off.'

Forty-two years after Smokeshell, he's had more than a hundred surgical procedures. There's a gaping, fist-sized wound where his sternum was and a colostomy bag is part of his everyday life.

But at first it was touch and go. One day he surfaced from the depths of anaesthesia to find Commandant Dippenaar and Cassie Schoeman (his company commander before Harmse took over) next to his hospital bed. HP had been Cassie's Ratel driver and they had a special relationship.

'Champ, you're going to make it,' Cassie told him. And HP answered: 'Oom Cassie, don't you worry, I'm going to live.'

He proved true to his word. For HP, the farm boy who cut hair and sold slap chips at boarding school and loved to run, had never heard of giving up.

At first, they kept his torn insides together with steel clamps, and he was in and out of surgery: 'Then it's to bind a bit of intestine, then it's to fix something else. As soon as I recovered sufficiently from one operation, they wheeled me in for the next one.'

He is in awe of surgeons like Professor Tielman Marais, who did the delicate work of repairing the horrific damage inflicted on the human body by heavy-calibre ammunition and jagged pieces of shrapnel: 'Think of it for a moment. Every day they were confronted with something they've never seen before … with cases like mine. That's not something any medical textbook could teach them.'

One concern was to ensure that his rectum would function normally, as his sphincter muscles had been blown away: 'Back then Prof Tielman said, "When I'm done, you'll be able to pinch a carrot in two," and he was right.' (Tragically, this would change after a botched procedure by another surgeon, years after HP was discharged from 1 Military Hospital.)

During his long hospital stay, HP was in constant agony: 'I would start screaming at night and they gave me a great deal of medication for pain, stress and I don't know what else. I was for ever swallowing pills or receiving injections.'

The strong medication came with a high risk of addiction: 'Sometimes they had to take me off something and then I had to be treated for the resulting withdrawal symptoms. It was a very difficult time.'

His injuries and condition were a great shock to his parents, who spent as much time next to his hospital bed as possible: 'It was really hard for them. You know, they lived on a farm near Theunissen in the Free State. It was a long way to travel and they knew nobody in Pretoria; they had to find a place to sleep.'

Weirdly, as HP got stronger and started moving around, life in hospital started to resemble that of a boarding school. Only there were nurses instead of teachers and prefects and at weekends his parents came to visit him, not the other way round.

'They would leave the farm every Saturday morning at 4 am and arrive at the hospital around 8 am. Then they would have a chat with everybody in the ward before we went out somewhere. But those days we did not know about restaurants; we were farm folks. So Dad just drove to some ordinary café.'

In the early months of surgery he was fed through a nasal tube. When he was able to eat independently again, he feasted on the food his mother brought from the farm kitchen: 'Boiled eggs, *frikkadelle* [meatballs] and especially cold *skaapnek* [mutton neck bones] … you carved the meat from the bones with a pocket knife. It all tasted so good.'

As time passed, he earned his *ouman* status in hospital, HP jokes: 'You could say I was promoted.' He was allowed to move from the big general ward to the smaller enclosed verandah, where all the long-term patients slept. Here these broken boys, some without limbs, were allowed to have their meals together. And at the head of the table presided HP in his wheelchair.

'Stoutgatte' (naughty buggers) is how he refers to himself and the other *oumanne* of Ward 2. For sometimes the goings-on were reminiscent of scenes from *M*A*S*H*, that dark television comedy about a US military field hospital during the Korean War.

Today he understands that the constant pranking and partying was a way of coping with the trauma of mangled bodies and emotional wounds: 'Ja, it was a form of self-therapy. I was a wild, naughty bugger in that hospital.'

Guys lying in traction were an easy target: 'When they're asleep you move one of those counterweights and prop it up on something. So when the guy stirs in his sleep the weight topples off and there's this sudden jerk on his foot … boy, did they get a fright! Sies, the terrible things we did.'

His locker was always stocked with whisky: 'I drank when I had to get off the pills. After lights out, the other guys came over and they always brought some bottles and we had a few good swigs. But you know, we did those things to stave off pity. If you allow yourself to feel sorry for a guy who lost his arm, you start feeling sorry for yourself. So you didn't. And that's how we helped each other.'

1 Military Hospital was a revolving door for the boys who sacrificed eyes, arms or legs on the altar of power politics. And when you're a resident patient for three years, you meet more than just a few of them: 'You know, there were three Bothas in that hospital. What were the chances? Sarel, Coenie and Renier and we all became friends.'

Behind every name on a bed chart there was a story linked to a specific 'incident' or operation. Like footnotes in the history of the Border War written in pain and blood. They were the stories of continued sacrifice and suffering hidden behind the headlines.

The hospital walls could not contain the *oumanne* of Ward 2. There was no leave in the official sense of the word, but they sneaked out in wheelchairs, on crutches and on artificial legs, the sighted sometimes leading the blind, for nights on the town: 'We just went, and at some stage they would discover you're not in the hospital.'

In a Spur or some such, they would drink it up. Sometimes things got out of hand and they were booted out: 'I think the hospital staff realised we were doing this to forget about our problems and disabilities. And they knew, after a night out, we would return and face the music.'

One member of this tight circle of long-term hospital inmates was 'old Sareltjie', who lost both legs in a terrible accident at 1 Parachute Battalion in Bloemfontein in 1981. Another recruit picked up an unexploded mortar bomb on the training field and carried this deadly souvenir into a crowded bungalow. He dropped it and it detonated. The blast killed three and wounded many others.

Sarel might have lost his legs but he had a car that he was allowed to keep on the hospital grounds. 'One of those hot little sporty numbers with a big slanted rear window,' recalls HP.

In the hospital's occupational therapy workshop, HP made Sarel a special 'driving foot'. He explains: 'You got this hard material that you soaked in warm water until you could mould it. So I shaped this wedge and attached it to the inside of Sarel's artificial leg with a bit of wood and with that he could operate the foot pedal of his automatic car.'

It was in Sarel's car that they fled the hospital and rolled their wheelchairs into some watering hole. When they returned to their home away from home, they were loud and obnoxious. And of course there were consequences, for even in these halls and wards a vestige of military order had to be maintained.

HP and his cronies were hauled before the hospital commander ('a brigadier or colonel, I can't remember his rank'). He lambasted and punished them, as was to be expected, but there was also a fatherly side to this senior officer who held sway over broken boys.

'Eventually he started taking us to rugby games over weekends, about four of us. Just so he could keep an eye on us. But we still drank and caused mayhem when we eventually got back to the hospital. And then you were in trouble once more.'

After one evening on the town, they were getting ready to go to bed when Sarel took the carafe of water on HP's bedside cabinet: 'I said, Sarel, leave my water alone, because I knew I would wake up at 1 or 2 am with a thirst.'

But the boozed-up Sarel challenged him: what are you going to do about it? HP answered: 'If you touch my water, I'll empty that colostomy bag (perched on a bedside cabinet) into your artificial leg.' And then chaos erupted.

Sarel produced a 9 mm pistol from his bedside drawer and started shouting that he was going to kill HP. 'I jumped out of my bed in a panic and started hobbling away with my walking sticks as fast as I could,' HP recalls.

Fortunately, the pistol was not loaded and there was no bloodshed. But in the pandemonium the colostomy bag on the bedside cabinet tipped over and the contents dribbled into Sarel's prosthetic limb after all. 'And boy, he never got that smell out of that leg. It honked like hell. After that we always teased him about his one *vrot voet* [rotten foot].' Eventually, the artificial leg was replaced by the hospital after Sarel damaged it beyond repair while working on his car – or so he claimed.

Nevertheless, Sarel and HP became the closest of friends. Sarel was discharged from the hospital before HP but still visited him and his parents regularly. Tragically, things eventually got too much for Sarel and he took his own life three years before the writing of this book.

James van Eck was another victim of the war who ended up in Ward 2. While on patrol in Ovamboland, his unit detonated a powerful landmine. Two identical twin brothers died together and James was blinded.

Again, it was the *ouman* of the ward who took James under his wing: 'James was brilliant at school, you know. He had Northern Transvaal colours for just about everything, from sport to debating. He wanted to study at university, but his parents were battling to cope ... All of a sudden, their brilliant child was blind and they did not know how to handle it.'

Finally, HP went over to James's parents and asked them what was going on, 'because old James misses you, he needs you'. It struck a chord, because after that they got more involved with their son and worked through things with him.'

At this stage, HP had his own small car on the hospital grounds and, in his pragmatic way, he started reintroducing James, who was raised in Pretoria, to the world outside Ward 2: 'I would drive through the city from south to north and read the street names out loud to James as we went. Then I would do the same from east to west ... criss-crossing the city centre and the area around the Tuks campus. All the while calling out the street names to him.'

One day, HP left the hospital for an altogether different reason. He was wheeled onto a military flight headed for Bloemfontein and then driven to 1 SAI. And there, for the first time since he had been almost cut in two in the Angolan bush, he was reunited with the other survivors of his platoon. Their two years were done and it was time to *klaar* out (the term used by both Afrikaans- and English-speaking SADF troops when referring to the end of their national service stint, from the Afrikaans 'uitklaar').

By that time, HP had already received his early discharge from the army on medical grounds. So he wore a civilian suit for the occasion and watched their final parade from a wheelchair. It was an emotional roller-coaster ride: 'I was very happy to see them again but I also teared up ... there were so few of them on parade, it was just heartbreaking.'

Then it was time for the final 'D-i-i-s ... MISSED!' before they were sent back to civvy street to carry on with their lives as if nothing had happened.

There were subdued hugs and handshakes then they scattered in all directions. HP, however, was flown back to Pretoria, as Ward 2 would remain his home for months to come.

By this time HP, James and the other *oumanne*, as well as all their parents, brothers and sisters, were like one big family. A visitor for one was a visitor for all. Sometimes the long-term patients would go out for dancing or dinner with the young resident nurses and physiotherapists. And there were regular weekend braais at the hospital: 'Sometimes we pushed our beds outside and slept by the fire under the stars. Those were healing moments for me.'

HP was now also allowed to leave the hospital for weekends on the family farm near Theunissen. He always invited a hospital buddy along.

Yes, they did talk to him about counselling: 'But I said, doctor, no need for that, I'll get along just fine. You see, back then I had no idea I had a psychological problem. I didn't even know what that meant.'

In time he would find out, however.

Then, 'sometime in 1982' and after almost three years in hospital, he was told it was time to go home. His wound was as healed up as it was going to get at that stage.

Saying goodbye to everyone was difficult: 'If you're sad to leave a hospital, you know you've been there far too long.'

But fate would be cruel and, as a result, he would see the inside of a hospital many more times.

It was time for a new chapter, but where to next? His long hospital stay had been difficult at times, but the hospital had also become a safe and familiar place.

HP had always wanted to work with his hands, so before his hospital discharge he inquired about joining the Permanent Force in order to learn a trade. But he was told he was now classified as G4K4 (medically unfit) and wouldn't be accepted.

His monthly SADF disability pension was a paltry R300 and he only had a practical Standard 8 certificate. But he refused to be a burden to his parents, so he had to hustle – just like the kid who once cut hair and sold slap chips at boarding school.

He discarded the wheelchair in favour of a walking stick, got into his father's battered old Datsun bakkie and drove from the farm to a well-known engineering firm in Bloemfontein. There, he told a man behind a desk: 'Oom, I don't have proper qualifications. But, see here, I got distinctions in maths, technical drawing and other subjects at school. Can't I draw plans for you?'

'Oom Coetzee', as HP would come to call him, clearly saw something in this young man who had just walked in off the street: 'He sat and looked at me for a few moments and then he told his secretary: "Annatjie, go show Hennie where to sit, he's starting work right now." And I replied, "I've only got the clothes I'm standing up in and no place to stay."'

That night he stayed with a friend in Bloemfontein, and the next morning he went back to the farm, packed his clothes and returned to the city to report to Oom Coetzee: 'And at that firm I worked my way up until I was basically a surveyor. I never had the qualifications on paper but I did the job regardless.'

One day in 1983, an angel came into his life. Phia, a brunette from Daniëlskuil, was a first-year student at the Bloemfontein Nursing College with a heart as big as the grassy Free State plains. It was her childhood dream to be a nurse. Her family could not afford a university education but she enjoyed the hands-on, practical approach the college offered.

'We had a hostel function,' she recalls, 'and I did not have a boyfriend at the time. But her friend Elize told her about this guy who was in hospital with her brother. 'I said okay, I don't believe in blind dates, but I didn't want to go the function alone.'

By agreement they met at the main post office in Bloemfontein. 'He was this skinny oke with longish hair covering his ears.'

At the hostel function they danced and then he took her to a roadhouse in his dad's old brown bakkie for a milkshake and a bite to eat. 'And ja, Hennie was apparently knocked off his feet but I can't say I felt anything for him at that stage.'

The next day, HP booked into the old Roberta Hotel, opposite the National Hospital, so he could take Phia dancing again: 'We just started spending more and more time together.' Eventually, he won her heart.

He never talked much about the war but was upfront about the medical consequences of his wound: 'My mother asked me if I was prepared to deal with all that and I said yes.'

They were married in 1984. 'But I'll tell you straight, I never realised what a difficult road lay ahead for us.'

Shortly after their wedding day, Phia completed her training. What she did not realise back then was that nursing would become a 24-hour occupation.

Certificate be damned, HP soon landed a surveyor's post at the Bloemfontein municipality. There, he was given the task of laying on water and sanitation to the black residential area just outside the Free State capital. As usual, he did things his own way.

'It was 1985 and I gave the unemployed an opportunity to earn something. Everything was done with pick and shovel, no machines were used.' His army of day workers got R2 for every metre of trench they dug, 'so if a guy dug five metres in one day he got R10.'

He tackled obstacles in his own way: 'When we got to a huge rock in the ground, we stacked old car tyres on top and burned

Phia and HP Ferreira in their youth.

HP showing off his catch.

them to heat the rock. Then we doused the rock with water until it cracked and we could remove it piece by piece.'

As he was finishing this project, the boss of a private engineering company pulled up, tossed the keys of a brand-new bakkie to him and said: 'Come work for me.' HP balked at first because he was loath to lose the housing subsidy he got from the municipality. But when he was offered three times his salary plus medical aid, he relented.

He worked hard: 'I always completed a contract ahead of the deadline. I was very hands-on, I clambered down the ditches and surveyed the levels myself.' Despite the constant pain caused by his war wound, he found pleasure in physical work, just as he did as a child on the farm. During his three years in hospital, he had learned that self-pity was the biggest enemy.

'It's like this: the guy who is deadly ill does not complain, he just lies there. Only the guy who is not all that ill has the strength to whine. And that's the gospel truth. Walk into any hospital and you'll see, the guy who complains is usually the guy they can't find any real fault with. But he keeps complaining, they keep finding nothing, and then he's back complaining again. And that makes me mad.'

When you listen to HP it's like the pain has become his motivation to live a positive and active live: 'I endure it because I want to carry on. I enjoy pressing those ceiling boards in place even though I'm hurting. Because I realise the reason for the pain I feel is that I'm doing something.

'But if you do nothing and still have pain, you start to question everything. Why did it happen? Better to carry on with your life and understand why it hurts in that moment.'

But as the physical wounds of Smokeshell continued to extract a

HP (left) strumming his guitar.

price, his suppressed emotional trauma would begin to resurface. HP would need his positivity and faith more than ever – and, above all, Phia's support.

From the day they were wed, tending to HP's wounds became as much a part of Phia's daily routine as brushing her teeth.

She got up at 4.30 am and spent about 45 minutes on HP's wound, cleaning and disinfecting. Then she drove to the hospital to start her shift. When she returned from the hospital, it was time to tend to HP again. Twice a day, every day. But all her loving care and the pills and injections could not banish his demons.

When Hennie (just about everybody else calls him HP, but for Phia he is her Hennie) fell quiet and retreated into himself, she knew he was in a dark place.

One of his passions was boeremusiek, she explains. He plays several instruments (his favourite guitar he built with his own hands) and got a band together: 'Even when he was physically hurting, he would sit down and play the organ for ten minutes.

Phia and her Hennie today.

And that told me he was okay. But some days he would not play at all and then I knew he was in a bad space. On those days he just wanted to lie down and sleep.'

Those bad patches usually started about two days before 10 June, the anniversary of the attack on Smokeshell: 'He was on his own planet and I learned to leave him be. I would wake him for a sandwich and tea and a hug, but apart from that I just gave him space.'

About two years into their marriage, HP took a hard look at himself. For three years in hospital he and his buddies from Ward 2 kept the demons at bay with their antics and drinking – but now all that was gone. He had to start managing his mental health on his own. Just like he did with everything else.

So he started talking to Phia about the war in broad terms, and she tried to support him as best she could: 'Okay, no way I could really understand what he went through in the army. But thanks to my passion to care for sick people, I could see he was hurting emotionally. I could acknowledge that and do what I could to ease his suffering.'

In his nightmares he once again saw the face of the Swapo gunner and the barrel of the 14,5 mil swinging towards him, followed by the sensation of a red-hot poker being thrust through his body. And on those nights, she would leave their marital bed and sleep elsewhere in the house: 'He would fight in his sleep so much that he could punch me with his fist without realising what he did.'

When the strain of living with his physical and emotional pain overwhelmed her, she would cry where he could not see or hear her. Alone. 'And I would pray to God to give me his pain for just one day so that Hennie would not have to endure it. Even for just one day.

'One day I told Hennie about that prayer and he said: "You won't be able to bear this pain, it's just too great a burden. But I thank God that you understand and that you want to help and that you are there for me."'

Before their wedding day, HP told Phia that the doctors had warned him he might never be able to conceive children. Phia was happy to deal with that issue in the long term but HP proved the doctors wrong. Their son, Henk, was born in 1990, followed by their daughter, Mariska, in 1992. They were overjoyed at the arrival of their kids, but HP's back was increasingly giving him hell.

'It was a very difficult time,' Phia confesses. 'The kids were very young and Hennie was in and out of hospital.'

HP's back was held together by surgical screws. And in 1992, shortly after Mariska's birth, he suffered a severe spasm due to pain, and some of the screws broke free. Phia explains what happened next.

'The protective film of tissue surrounding his spinal marrow tore and his spinal fluid started leaking out. As a result he suffered severe headache and disorientation.'

He was back in hospital for two weeks and she had to look after their two babies by herself. Tragically, the operation to fuse his vertebrae was not as successful as hoped. Phia reached the point where she asked God to hasten the Day of Reckoning so that everybody, HP included, could be relieved of their earthly suffering and pain.

After pouring out her heart in prayer, she got off her knees and carried on, because Hennie and the kids needed her.

After his discharge from hospital, HP was pushed around construction sites in a wheelchair in order to make sure the job was done right. He got through it with the help of pain pills and his usual grit. In a bizarre way the hurting was good, for the satisfaction of working made the pain worthwhile.

But eventually, 'just before 1994', he was medically discharged from his job and another difficult time followed. The daily regime of pain pills and other medication he needed to keep going was expensive, not to mention more surgical procedures. To pay for all this, he took a second mortgage on their home.

And, true to his nature, he never stopped hustling and making plans. One such plan was an invention that made that icon of the South African veld, the *windpomp* (windmill), easier to maintain. Basically, HP explains, he invented a *windpomp kop* that ran on ball bearings, and he patented it: 'So any farmer could maintain it, because he could buy those ball bearings from the local co-op once the gear was cut to fit.'

For a while, HP was a bit like the 'windpomp ingenieur' of Laurika Rauch's popular Afrikaans song 'Die Ballade van Jacob F de Beer': 'I converted about 156 windmill heads. And if a farmer needed a complete windmill, I built and erected it for him.'

Mariska, still young and with fingers small enough to reach the difficult spots, pushed bolts through holes so HP could fasten them. Sometimes his son, Henkie, then in Grade 8, lent a hand, and there was one full-time worker.

They would load the tower on the back of his old bakkie with six feet of steel framework protruding front and back. The big round head would be propped on its side. 'And then we would go and erect it and that was that.'

His windmill patent paid his medical bills but his daily care was still in Phia's loving hands. Sometimes concerned friends asked her where she found the strength to tend to Hennie after a long shift at the hospital.

'Yes, it can feel as if you're never off duty,' she admits in her candid manner. 'But you know, he did not bring this on himself, he did not ask to be wounded in this manner. He believes we were destined to meet because he needed somebody who understands about sickness and suffering, and so do I.

'I really love Hennie, he is my whole life. I love being with him, just to talk or rub his back when he's not feeling well. I believe all this suffering brought us closer together and closer to God.'

For many years after leaving the military hospital, HP had no contact with the other survivors of that day of fire and blood in the Angolan bush.

And he did not really want to reconnect, he admits today: 'I believed it would drag me back emotionally to the place where I was hurt, that I would relive it all. The mere thought scared me.'

But now and then he would bump into a fellow Smokeshell veteran while going about his daily business. Eventually, he started to believe it would be a good thing to get together. And sometime in 2007, the feelers started going out.

Plans were made to gather in Bloemfontein on 10 June, the anniversary of the attack, to honour their fallen brothers. It was HP who tracked down his former platoon commander in George and telephoned him: 'I begged Paul to come, even if I had to fetch him in George myself and drive him back to Bloemfontein. And ja, old Paul came and here he started opening up.'

In a way, this first reunion filled the gap left by the brotherhood of wounded and disabled in Ward 2: 'It was about guys who went through the same thing getting together and talking about it.'

It would become an annual event in a corner of Tempe Military Base, where they first reported for their national service and took the first step on the road to Smokeshell. Some veterans joined in from the word go but others resisted all efforts to draw them into the circle.

These memorial services are deeply emotional. When HP kneels to lay his wreath at the base of the small memorial, he feels the physical presence of all those who were lost: 'It is like you still can't believe they're all dead.'

During these events he also relives the moment he was shot, and the bitter smell and taste of burned flesh: 'But ja, I'm grateful that I can pay my respects to them every year. Because I believe, in order to heal, you have to get the guys who went through that kind of thing together to talk about it. Whatever operation you were in, go find somebody who was also there. Your tears will wash your emotional wounds.'

But what about the enemy's dead? 'We were not guilty of murder, we were soldiers ordered to do a job. In all honesty, I did not really know what we were going to do. I was young and full of life and wanted to do something for my country. You didn't know whether it was right or wrong, you just did it and gave it your all.'

Many young troopies at Smokeshell were puzzled to find Bibles and family photographs when they went through the uniform pockets of dead Swapo soldiers as ordered. This did not quite match the narrative of godless, murdering communists that they had been taught. Suddenly, the enemy seemed as human as any of the boys from South Africa's farms and cities.

But HP, who was wounded so quickly and casevaced the same day, only got that insight many years later. He and Phia were on a bus to the airport after a television show in Johannesburg. One of their fellow passengers was a former enemy who had also participated in the TV discussion. Hennie turned to Phia and wondered out loud who this 'so-and-so' thought he was. 'Then he said to me: "Nee man, Hennie, ek kan Afrikaans verstaan!" So we started talking and I realised he was just a soldier and human being like me.'

At that moment, he had no idea that one day he would return to the place in the Angolan bush where his young, healthy body was shattered, in order to honour the dead of all sides. A journey to heal the mind and thereby help the flesh endure.

10
MARCO AND PAMELA

The first thing Marco saw when he regained consciousness was the looming bulk of Oshakati's water tower, framed in the window against the backdrop of a pale yellow sunrise.

He felt the almost forgotten sensation of crisp bed linen against his skin: 'I was in my underpants and my head hurt like hell, but I realised, "I've made it, I'm still alive."'

Then his mind's eye forced him to see his friend Robert de Vito lying dead next to the Ratel. Rob, who on the eve of the battle spoke to Marco of his fear that he would not survive.

'All I could think of in that sick bay bed was, "What am I going to tell his parents?"'

It was the morning after the attack on Smokeshell and Marco had yet to hear how many others in his section and platoon had been killed and wounded: 'I remember somebody was brought in on a stretcher and I heard a medic say: "Caforio is also here." And then I heard Martin French say, "No, Caforio's dead, he cracked completely." I listened to Martin sobbing in that ward, not knowing I was still alive.'

Marco was under heavy sedation and could not call out or go to Martin.

After two days in Oshakati's sick bay, he was transferred to

Grootfontein and there he glimpsed Martin again for a brief second: 'There was this curtain around his bed and they were inserting a catheter. Then we were past and I still could not tell him I was alive.'

Marco's bladder had not worked for three days owing to shock and the medics wanted to insert a catheter into him as well: 'But I begged the nurse not to and eventually they left me alone with a bedpan. After battling for five minutes I managed to wet the whole bed, but they just said, "Don't worry, don't worry."'

When he was stable enough, he too embarked on the final leg of the aerial casevac route – from Grootfontein to 1 Military Hospital in Pretoria: 'It was the old hospital building, not the new one. I could not believe how many operational casualties there were, many from Smokeshell. In the bed next to mine was a black soldier from 32 Battalion who was hit in the face by a mortar. But it did not explode, there was just this hole. I can't remember if he lived or died.'

HP was also there. 'And Pottie from section 1, with shrapnel wounds. Also Paul Louw with burn wounds.' He has a vivid memory of Paul, clad in a blue-and-white-striped hospital dressing gown, visiting each of his wounded troops and crying by their bedside. And for the first time Marco heard that 13 of their company had been killed and 26 wounded.

Some of the wounded were discharged after less than a week, but Marco ended up staying for four months. Each day he had to endure the agony of the nursing staff cleaning his shrapnel wounds. Tiny pieces in his eye socket and hand could not be removed, and he needed physiotherapy for his hand after it stiffened partially.

'Every night HP screamed in agony. He would shout, "Caforio, get the nurse please, I'm in pain." When I started moving around in a wheelchair, I would go to his bed to talk and he showed me the massive hole in his back.'

Eventually Marco and Martin French, who at first thought he was dead, were discharged together. As their company was still in Ovamboland, they were sent from the hospital to 1 SAI.

To walk into the Bloemfontein training base, with its rigid discipline, after all they'd been through, was unpleasant: '"Wie's julle?" [Who are you?] is how they greeted us. We tried to explain we were just discharged from hospital after we were wounded in Smokeshell. But they would not believe we were wounded and we were accused of going AWOL [absent without leave].

'Just walking normally was difficult enough, but those corporals made us march in place. Eventually we had to go on orders in front of the colonel, and that was when French cracked. He just started shouting, "Fuck this army, I've had enough!" I tried to silence him but he kept shouting fuck this, fuck that … I think that was the last straw for him.'

The end of the matter was that they were given a choice: stay at 1 SAI or go back to the Border to rejoin Bravo Company. It was an easy choice for them and they could not leave that place fast enough. Yet the journey back north – by air to Grootfontein and then by road to Omuthiya – was an unsettling experience, Marco admits.

Platoon 1 as they knew it did not exist anymore and they were assigned to one of the three remaining platoons: 'But all the guys came to us and embraced us, told us they were glad we made it and that they were sorry about Rob … It was a good feeling.'

It was the start of November and they would stay with the company until everybody was discharged together that December: 'We did not go out on patrol with the guys, we just hung around at Omuthiya. But the strange thing was, nobody ever asked us about what we had gone through, about how bad it was. Nobody talked about it.'

Back on the parade ground in Bloemfontein, their discharge parade, usually a joyful occasion, was a sombre affair. There was a moment of silence for their friends who would never be going home, and that was it.

Marco and some of the guys carpooled back to Johannesburg and civvy street. The long journey passed in silence. Nobody felt like heroes. They were merely survivors; their dead buddies were the heroes.

One thing they loudly agreed on – they wanted fuck-all more to do with the army.

Marco's parents had a hard time dealing with what happened to the son they had entrusted to the army of their adopted country. They sold their Johannesburg pizzeria and home, and the family returned to Italy.

In the Tuscan city of Pisa, renowned for its leaning tower and medieval architecture, they bought a small inn: 'So I went from the heat of Angola to the snow of Italy ... but things did not work out and six months later we were back in South Africa.'

It was a year later, he says, 'that things went to hell, I would just lie under my bed screaming.' In his mind he was back in Angola and the Ratel spattered with the blood of his mutilated friends.

'My dad said, this is crap, I gave them my son and this is how they give him back to me. So together we went to Pretoria to take on the brass hats and finally the army arranged counselling and gave me a pension.'

Like HP, his medical status was downgraded to unfit for military service. But even so the Regiment Johannesburg tried to call him up for a Citizen Force camp during this time. When they could not find him, they wanted to have him arrested, Marco recalls wryly.

For the next year he reported to the medical faculty at Wits University for monthly counselling sessions: 'My shrink was Commandant Le Roux. We talked and she gave me medication and even hypnotised me. She always said I would never forget what I went through, but in time I would heal. And it's true, you have to learn to be strong … but for the first five years after the war I drank and cried and fought a lot.'

Unlike many veterans, he did not balk at talking about his experiences 'because I was young and stupid and I thought it would help my healing'. But that changed one night in 1981: 'I was at a braai with friends and we were drinking. They started asking me about the army, and while I was talking I heard one of my friends say: "Ag, there he goes again with his war stories, what movies has he been watching?" I just swung around and moered him. From that moment I stopped talking about it. When somebody asked me about my injuries, I told them a pressure cooker exploded.'

Marco was not the only one who made up stories to explain his injuries, he would later hear. Martin French, who lost his leg when the 23 mil punched holes in their Ratel, moved to the coast after they were discharged from the army. So he just told people he was a shark-bite victim.

Marco did, however, keep his promise to his dead friend. He went so see Robert de Vito's parents in Boksburg. Rob's father has since passed away, but Marco stayed in contact with his mother and younger sister.

'Rob's death broke his mother's heart. She is 84 now but time has not made the loss any easier to bear. We phone each other and she tells people I'm her other son and her daughter's big brother.'

Marco got on with his life. He worked as a motor mechanic, met and married his first wife and had three children. Still, the echoes of war refused to fade away. But then deliverance came from out of the blue in every sense of the word.

As a national serviceman, Marco had tried and failed to become a paratrooper. But his brother Fabricio, known as Fuz, had taken to recreational parachuting. And one day in 1987 Fuz said: 'Come on Marco, come and jump with me.' So he did – and he could not wait for the next time.

'When I was in therapy my shrink, the commandant, actually told me I needed to do something to get my adrenaline pumping. Turns out she was right all along.'

Pretty soon he was hooked: 'You're nervous when you stand in the open doorway of that aircraft before you jump. Your stomach is fluttering. But it's a good sensation, it's not fear. I flippen love the rush. My first jump was with a static line, and after Fuz and I hit the ground we just never stopped jumping. Man, it keeps me going.'

Together, he and Fuz qualified to do free fall then they started a skydiving team that competes nationwide. The intricate aerial aerobatics and formations of the sport have become a rhythm of his life.

They named the skydiving team 'The United Nations' in honour of the section that was wiped out at Smokeshell.

Marco also found release in music. His band, Paradox, played the pubs and restaurants of the West Rand and East Rand. Just like HP's band in Bloemfontein. But while HP loved boeremusiek, city boy Marco stayed faithful to the rock music he listened to

Marcio Caforio ready for another jump.

in the days before Smokeshell. Pink Floyd, Deep Purple ... the music of thundering drums and guitars roaring and weeping.

Yes, the skydiving and the band helped his healing a great deal. But there was still one big step he had to take, he admits today.

Of her own background Pam knows very little. She and her brother were adopted at a very young age by a Roodepoort family and never knew their biological parents. When she was only nine, her adoptive parents divorced.

'After 14 years as a housewife my mom had to go get a job to keep a roof over our heads and put food in our stomachs. She never remarried and basically worked seven days a week, but here we are today.'

Marco's first marriage was history when he accompanied Fuz

Marco and Pamela Caforio today.

to a friend's funeral, where he met Pam. 'After that he just would not leave me alone! For the next six months he pestered me for a date,' she recalls.

At last she said, what the hell, and they went to Gold Reef City. And that was the start of their life together.

Pam is a no-nonsense women who tells it like it is, but she has a big heart. Her sons may have left the roost but her eight pugs, all rescue dogs, have the run of the place.

She and Marco will tell you that their marriage was not always smooth sailing.

'The big thing is love,' says Marco. 'And that thing they call "for better or for worse". Look, we had our struggles but we've been married for 30 years, so something is right. You just have to work at it. Because I've got my moods, you know.'

Those moods surfaced every year around 10 June, when the emotional shrapnel of Smokeshell started hurting. For three, four days at a time he would fall silent and withdraw from everybody around him. Pam would just leave him be until he felt like talking again, something he appreciates: 'She always supported me and never moaned when I went skydiving or to play with the band.'

Early in their marriage, Smokeshell once more took a physical toll. Doctors removed all the shrapnel they could find but a minuscule piece at the back of his eye socket remained. The fluid started leaking from his eye 'and it dried up like a raisin', as Marco puts it.

They were living in a one-bedroomed flat in Johannesburg when severe pain and blurred vision signalled that something was seriously wrong. Pam ran down the stairs to the café below and asked to use the phone to call Marco's doctor.

Marco was in surgery for eight hours and eventually his eye was removed. Their son was two years old at the time. 'So, ja, it was difficult,' says Pam. 'But together we hung in there and got through all of that. Marco has only one eye but it never stopped him doing something.'

One day in 2007, he was sitting in a restaurant when his phone rang and a voice from the past said: "We're going to have a Smokeshell reunion in Bloem, would you like to come?" 'I said no, I don't want to know anything about the army; that part of my life is over.'

For he remembered that night around the braai fire when his friend openly mocked him. And he remembered the words of his friend Kelvin Luke, who had saved his life so long ago: 'The guys who experienced all these things usually stay quiet while those who did nothing do all the talking. So when the guys who were really there *do* speak up, people think they're talking kak.'

He went to Pam and told her about the phone call. And she said:

'No, Marco, I think we should go. It could be a good thing.' She convinced him and he started feeling excited.

Pam went along to that first informal gathering: 'It was an unbelievable experience. I'll never forget it. I think there were maybe 13 people and I was the only woman. You know, Marco never talked about the army and the war, just like most men, until he got reunited with other 61 Mech veterans. If they did not meet that day, they would probably still not be talking about it.'

She was deeply moved by what she saw when the men started talking about the past: 'Grown men were openly crying, all of them. There was not a dry eye in that room. Old wounds were reopened but the healing also began.'

In the dining room of their Weltevredenpark home, they send their impressions of that first *skouerskuur* (as 61 vets call these gatherings, meaning 'to rub shoulders') flying across the table like ping-pong balls.

Marco: 'You know, after we were shot, and up to the day we klaared out, nobody talked about it, we just went our separate ways. And for the first time, after so many years, we were all telling each other what happened to us, what our piece of the story was. HP, Paul Louw, myself and the other guys. For the first time you heard what really happened to the other guys of your platoon. All the kak we went through that nobody talked about. And it took all those years to get it out.'

Pam: 'When you keep it bottled up inside, it affects everybody around you. Yes, it was the apartheid era and all that, the history and all that, but why can't they talk about it, why this great silence? When it all stays inside it just leads to bitterness.'

It was also Pam who reached out to Martin French before the Bloem event. Marco had told her earlier that Martin wanted nothing to do with the army, but Pam tracked him down, phoned him and convinced him it would be a good thing to talk to his old buddies: 'And he dropped everything and flew to Bloem. They talked all night and when he went to bed that night he experienced ghost pains for the first time.' (Amputees sometimes feel a pain or itch as if the limb is still there, but the pain is psychosomatic – there is no actual physical sensation.) Pam believes he had to face his trauma before experiencing the ghost pains and subsequent emotional healing.

Marco: 'Yes, everybody opened up, even Paul. Before that day I never knew how he was wounded, how Venter died and what happened when he pulled Fourie off the Ratel … It was a great shock to hear what actually happened to the whole platoon.'

Pam stayed involved. When the newly founded 61 Mech Veterans Association (61 MVA) held its first annual memorial day at the National Museum of Military History in Johannesburg (for all 61 Mech vets, not only Smokeshell participants), she was at Marco's side. And she volunteered her time to record and type the stories of these former warriors for the 61 MVA website.

She stresses: 'It all started with that first tiny gathering in Bloemfontein. And today there are hundreds who attend the annual memorial day in Johannesburg and regional *skouerskure* all over the country. Everything has come out in the open.'

Marco confirms what Pam says: 'The more you talk to other guys who were there and went through the same kind of thing, the more you heal. You start talking and then you just get better and better.'

He is now also a long-standing member of the Memorable Order of Tin Hats (MOTH), an organisation founded after World War I to support veterans the world over. But in South Africa the MOTH 'shellholes' (as branches are called) have become a safe

The names of the Smokeshell dead on the 61 Mech memorial, which was moved from Omuthiya to the War Museum in Johannesburg after the Border War.

space for Border War veterans: 'You talk to guys who understand because they were there. I will never forget what I experienced but it gets better, one step at a time. And that's how it is.'

In 2010, Marco had his say on national television, with HP and Paul. The opportunity arose in the context of a documentary on trauma put together by the writer Rian Malan and TV presenter Ruda Landman. There was a moment when Marco pointed his finger at the camera and addressed the generals and politicians: 'You used us and then just left us, you did not even give us medals.'

A few weeks after the programme, their medals arrived in the mail. 'You know what, it's for my sons, so that they could know what I did,' he says.

But the last word on this comes from Pam: 'Marco always says those who did not come home are the real heroes. But to me they are all heroes. Those who came home and those who didn't. And Marco too.'

It was 2018 when Marco finally embarked on a physical journey back to Angola.

It's hard to explain just how extraordinary that trip was. More than a hundred 61 Mech veterans and a number of their wives and children, from all over South Africa, converged in Windhoek before driving up through Namibia and crossing into Angola. Former commanders of 61 Mech also participated.

The convoy of bakkies and Land Rovers braved Angola's bone-rattling roads for about a fortnight in order to visit the many battlefields of 61 Mech's war. Time and again, senior Angolan military officers, bureaucrats and villagers turned out to welcome them. Lavish feasts were laid on for the former invaders from the south, and during joint memorial services for the fallen many a tear was shed. And all the while Marco, Kelvin Luke and a handful of other Smokeshell veterans yearned also to revisit the site of their bloodiest day.

But it was not meant to be. Every major battlefield was visited except Smokeshell. Why? Because nobody knew where it was. Just about every other famous battleground – from Protea to Askari and Cuito Cuanavale – was well charted because of the towns, rivers, bridges and significant roads that served as landmarks and reference points. But Smokeshell had none of these. It seemed like the bush itself had swallowed it to keep its location secret.

Finally, the Smokeshell guys, a close-knit tribe in the larger community of veterans, accepted they were not going to find it this time. Under a tree next to a deserted airstrip, they held a small memorial service of their own. It was hundreds of kilometres away from where it all happened so long ago, but at least it was on Angolan soil. They left crosses for their fallen friends and knelt in prayer with their arms around each other. 'Jeez, it was so emotional,' Marco says.

During that Angolan trip he felt no rancour towards the former enemy. 'Maybe because I was so much older, you change as the years go by. Their job was to fight, the same as us. It was good to embrace and shed tears with them. They treated us like kings.

'Politicians declared that war, not us. We did what we had to do and so did they. Maybe we were just young and stupid. But that is all in the past and we are older and wiser.'

But, like many other veterans, 'I do not regret anything, I am proud of what I did. Sadly, there are always casualties when you go to war. Some die, some are wounded, some go home without a scratch. It's all about how you handle things ... The army taught me how to handle the difficult things in life.'

He respects the guys who do not want anything to do with the past, those who told the army to shove their medals where the sun don't shine. His medals, he stresses, are for his sons to remember what he did after he is gone.

Today he lives to jump, for his wife, his music and the sons who make him so proud. And he is silent no more. When the fakers and posers, those who are not the real deal, start running off at the mouth, he looks them in the eye and says, 'My man, you've done fuck-all.'

Pam keeps him real in her own no-nonsense way. She's done three static-line jumps herself just to get a feel for what he loves. But when he goes off for a day of free falling through the blue skies, she enjoys a day at home alone. Just doing stuff in her garden. 'If he didn't go skydiving, he would probably drive me nuts.'

She doesn't join him for the big annual get-togethers anymore, but helping Marco to break his silence and unburden has given her new insights into who he is. 'Yes, she was there for me from the start,' Marco confirms.

Sometimes she attends a gig and takes to the dance floor with the other wives and girlfriends while the band plays. But Marco knows: when he goes off by himself to skydive or play, don't come home at two in the morning. Then there'll be trouble.

Not that Marco has any wish to get up to that kind of nonsense. He knows and appreciates the value of his wife and best friend and understands the importance of mutual respect and understanding: 'You know, I'm 64 and she is 52 and the kids are gone. There's no room for the bullshit of the past, we only look ahead. It's just the two of us now.'

Oh, and also the eight tail-wagging orphans Pam just had to adopt.

11
PAUL AND LYNETTE

The black haze over the battlefield dwindled to a thin smear then disappeared as the helicopter scudded over the bush to the south. Finally, the aircraft dropped from the sky and crouched down on the Grootfontein runway.

Throughout its known history, Grootfontein has been a crossroads. First came the San and other indigenous peoples such as the Damara, Herero and Ovambo. The Afrikaners known as the Dorsland Trekkers followed, then the *Schutztruppe* of the German colonial government. And now it was the great revolving door of the Border War, where transport aircraft disgorged fresh troops from the States before loading up with *oumanne* for the trip back home.

The military hospital at Grootfontein was also an important stop on the air ambulance route. Here, critical medical procedures were done to stabilise the seriously wounded before the long haul to Pretoria. And it was at the Grootfontein military hospital that Paul Louw spent a deeply disturbing night: 'You just see wounded guys coming in round the clock and young surgeons packing up due to lack of sleep and exhaustion. You hear a doctor say, "I can't carry on" and see him turn around and walk away … that kind of thing.'

A few of his wounded troops were also there, but the worst cases like HP and Marco had already been rushed onwards to

1 Military Hospital outside Pretoria, 1,500 km to the southeast. All too soon, Paul joined them there.

Those two or three weeks in 1 Mil can never be erased from his memory. Nights were filled with the screams of men in pain or tortured by nightmares: 'Some were my own troops and you had to wrestle them down on the floor to stop them from running through a glass door or something. And hold them down until the nursing staff could tranquillise them. These were things I've never seen before and I started thinking, "Hell, am I going to turn out the same way?"'

In years to come he would indeed wake up sweating from his own nightmares, followed by the great relief that he was in his bed and not back in a burning Ratel or in the Angolan bush surrounded by his dead or dying men. Thankful that he was not out of his mind, that he was 'dealing with it'.

Many years would pass before he realised he was not dealing with it as well as he liked to think. The one big difference between him and some of his troops? He was able to function, to carry on with his life. But all that was still in the future on the day he said goodbye to HP, Marco and other patients and walked out of 1 Mil.

About five of Paul's troops were discharged on the same day as him. They were on their way back to Ovamboland and 61 Mech, but their first stop was at 1 SAI in Bloemfontein. When Paul got there, the training unit was on parade, 'and I fell in with the light duties and odds and sods at the back because all of a sudden you're a nobody'.

But two senior officers who were father figures to Paul immediately spotted him. One was Ep van Lill, the man who had shaped Paul into a mechanised platoon commander. The other was Cassie Schoeman, the commander of Bravo Company until three months before the attack on Smokeshell.

'They simply walked across the parade ground and pulled me out of that squad of odds and sods and took me to Oom Ep's office. And Cassie asked me, with tears in his eyes, "What happened to my boys?" And I told him: "Exactly what you told us and what you trained us for ... Things happened, shots were fired and a lot of guys died."'

Paul's initial bravado soon evaporated as he relived the battle for Cassie and Ep. It was intensely emotional for the men crowded into that office so far from the battlefield.

'You know, I never knew my father. But I was fortunate to have other father figures in my life. And Cassie was one of them, he made such a difference, he was such a positive influence. I call him my "Bloemfontein dad". Up to this day, years after the war, we get emotional when I call him on the phone.'

But that conversation in Ep's office was not the end of it. After a military operation there's always a formal autopsy. What did we do right, what did we do wrong? What do we have to do better next time, what do we need to change? Because lessons learned in blood are hugely expensive and must not be taken lightly.

One of the many issues under the magnifying glass was the aviation fuel for the choppers that was left behind. This meant the parabats could not be deployed to cut off Swapo's escape routes and kill as many of the enemy as possible. And it was over this issue that Paul went head to head with one of the big guns of the army, Colonel (later General) Witkop Badenhorst, during the formal review of the attack on Smokeshell.

'He said I was responsible, that it was my job to see that the chopper fuel was carried to Mulemba in Angola on the back of a logistics truck. But I said no, that's not true, in the operational orders it was clearly stated that he (Badenhorst) was to organise it, but he never did. And he replied: "Are you calling me a liar?" And I said: "Colonel, with all due respect, yes. You are lying."'

The end of this exchange was that General Constand Viljoen – the man who sat Paul down in Angola after the battle and convinced him he could do more by joining his wounded men in the States – gave Badenhorst a keyholder in the shape of a tiny fuel drum as a souvenir. This humorous gesture symbolised a small personal victory for Paul.

Also under severe scrutiny was the outdated intelligence provided to Dippenaar to plan his assault, the air force bombardment three days before the ground force moved in, and Paul's decision not to do reconnaissance on foot before his Ratels drove out of the dry riverbed.

But, like Dippenaar has said many times since, Paul was the only one there. And despite the hell that Platoon 1 had to fight through, they achieved their objectives.

'We may have suffered less casualties if different decisions had been made,' Paul says today. 'But I believe we did well against a far greater force and we inflicted a great many enemy casualties.'

Then it was time for the flight back to Grootfontein, and from there by road up past Etosha and on to Omuthiya. For Paul, the return to the base under the camelthorn trees was strange and difficult. All his troops had been alive and well the last time he'd been there, but now only half turned out to greet him. And after the meat grinder of Smokeshell, the days seemed to drag by pointlessly.

'You know, a big chunk was torn out of Bravo Company and the guys felt broken, I think. It was a bad time and there was a lot of negativity in the air. We were basically just kept busy for the last two or three months until we klaared out.'

Keeping busy meant patrolling the Ovambo trust area known as the Mangetti Block and the farms of the Tsintsabis region to the north of Omuthiya. On one patrol in this vast expanse of white sand and thorny bush, they came upon a terrified Ovambo woman in labour. Paul and Gareth Rutherford, who had to watch helplessly while his friends died at Smokeshell, helped to bring her baby into the world.

The bond between Paul and his surviving troops was still there: 'When we got back together again, we clicked just like before.' But they did not talk much about what they had gone through in Angola and even less about the guys whose names were not heard at roll call anymore. 'I just think nobody wanted to get drawn into discussions about that kind of stuff.'

At Omuthiya, Paul was reunited with another survivor of that hell in the Angolan bush: the puppy he 'liberated' from a Swapo bunker. 'The day I arrived back at the base the troops came to me and said, "Here, this is your dog." They named him Smokie.'

When the day arrived to shake the powdery dust of Ovamboland off their boots for the last time as national servicemen, Smokie was not left behind: 'During the flight back to Bloemfontein he was in my backpack. I let my mother know when we were due to land, and when we walked off the aircraft I gave the dog to her and asked her to look after it. There was no time for explanations as we were hustled onto vehicles and driven off.'

They spent the last month or so of their army stint 'somewhere on the Orange River, in the vicinity of Smithfield or maybe Gariep. Doing a bit of training with live ammo, fishing and swimming. Nothing hectic.'

The triggers of trauma were ever present in the glowing red heart of a braai fire or the thick, cloying stench of diesel, but everybody clammed up about whatever they were feeling. For Paul, it was the start of what he would later call his 'silent time' – the time of not talking about his feelings.

That silence would last for 28 years.

After leaving the army, Paul adapted to life on civvy street without great difficulty. This, he believes, was because he grew up in a disciplined household. The discipline of a commandant and father he never knew, but also the discipline of a mother who had to raise her kids alone. And this was the environment he returned to with his discharge papers in his pocket: 'So I did not have to start over. I just returned to the home environment I knew and understood and carried on.'

He started working at becoming the man he had heard so many good things about – his father, the officer and academic. Paul studied city planning at the University of the Orange Free State and plunged back into the melee of rugby.

'I was never a very clever rugby player … I was the big midfielder who just crash-tackled everybody,' he claims. Yet he was good enough to run out for Shimlas, as the varsity side was known, in the company of a number of future provincial stars.

Outwardly, he was an easygoing, jovial guy who enjoyed a pint and a laugh with his mates. Somebody who was not held back by the traumatic events of the past, or who reverted to alcoholism, drugs or even suicide, as some war veterans do. He was functioning, he told himself, he was 'handling things' and moving on with his life.

Today, he realises that maybe he was not handling things all that well. 'What I was doing was avoiding confrontation. Whenever conflict of any kind loomed, I withdrew. And when I did not pull back, I became very aggressive,' he admits all these years later at his home in George.

Back then he simply ignored emotional triggers such as fire and the smell of diesel and kept his mouth shut about what was behind him. Only after two failed marriages and the loss of a very special friend would he start to confront the past.

Paul married the sister of an army friend while he was still a student. She was 'a splendid person' but their marriage lasted only four years. After that he got seriously involved with another girl he met on campus. When he graduated and accepted a job offer from the town planning department of George, the couple tied the knot and moved to the Garden Route. They had a son but divorced after a year.

'And then it was a case of third time lucky for me.'

Lynette Louw was still at school in Kempton Park when she learned to fight for those she loved.

Back then, diagnosis of learning impairments and other mental challenges – not to mention awareness and sensitivity – was sadly lacking. And school could be an especially cruel environment for kids who were labelled 'slow'. Lynette's older brother was one of those kids whose challenges were not even remotely understood.

'At school he was always mocked as that stupid kid, that crazy kid,' she recalls. Lynette went at her brother's tormentors like a wildcat.

'I would get home from school with the sleeves ripped off my blouse, a bloodied nose and blackened eye. Because I fought the boys and told them my boetie is *not* crazy, he can't help how he is.

'When I got to Grade 1 my brother was still there after two or maybe three years. We shared the same classroom but he was made to sit right at the back with a round sticker on his forehead, what they called *die esel* [the donkey], as they used to do with the so-called dumb kids. And I sat right at the front, with a gold star for being smart ... For three years I taught him to read, because he was beaten every time he made a mistake while reading in class.'

It would be years before her brother was correctly diagnosed. But until then he was under Lynette's wing. 'So we walked that road together ... because I could manage things that he could not.'

This feeling of responsibility towards her brother she calls her *saamdra-gevoel* (to carry a burden together). 'And maybe that's why Paul and I ended up together.'

She was also previously married – to a medical student she met while studying physiotherapy at Stellenbosch University. After they graduated, they had a somewhat nomadic life in the bushveld before he accepted a post at the state hospital in George and she got a job at a private practice. They had two children before they divorced, but she stayed on in George.

By this time, Paul's second divorce was behind him and he was working his way up through the officer ranks in the local area commando – just like his father before him. And he was still playing rugby for a George side, which is why he needed the services of a physiotherapist one day in 1991.

As Paul tells it, she treated his injury and they became friends: 'And one day she asked me to look after her kids while she went out ... Her trust made a huge impression on me.'

True to her nature, Lynette has a more down-to-earth version of events.

'Paul had a broken finger and the orthopaedic surgeon wanted to find me a husband, so he sent Paul to me for treatment. Okay, so we got to know each other ...'

As their relationship progressed, they moved in together, and that was just fine for both of them. 'My divorce was very traumatic and I did not want to go down that road again,' Lynette explains.

It made no difference to Paul, but the Dutch Reformed Church did not approve. The dominee turned up at their door and threatened to boot them out if they continued to live outside wedlock. The kids would also be barred from attending Sunday school.

So they arranged to be married by a magistrate friend in their home. Only six people were in attendance. (They would have a proper bash with lots of friends and family at a later stage.) 'Paul and the magistrate had had a bit of a skinful by the time the ceremony started,' Lynette recalls with wry humour. 'So if ever I wanted to have this marriage nullified, I could argue that both of them were drunk!'

She soon realised that the not-so-gentle shove from the dominee was all for the best: 'It gives you stability. I always told my kids that simply living together was a lot of fun, but you don't share everything. You're always on your toes, on your best behaviour. But once you're married you let go a bit.'

But it would be another five years before Paul broke his silence about the war.

'You know, when I met Paul he was a really jovial guy. I never realised that he suffered trauma, that he was carrying a burden. He was just always happy. He played rugby, enjoyed hanging out with a big circle of friends ... just a normal guy. It was a very happy time.

'He told me a bit about Smokeshell once but just in the broadest of terms, not how bad it really was. And he showed no emotion when he talked about it. He basically said this is what happened and it's over and done with and never talked about it again.'

As they settled into married life, however, she started to notice that at times he would withdraw for no apparent reason: 'When I asked him about it, he would just say, "Nothing, it's nothing." The more I asked, the more he withdrew.'

But it would never be that easy to shrug off Lynette. There was her childhood as her brother's fierce guardian angel, and she had studied psychology in order to qualify as a physiotherapist. She had a way of seeing and understanding things: 'Paul needs recognition. He wants to feel that he is doing the right thing, that he is handling stuff the proper way. Only later would I realise this was probably because of Smokeshell. He's forever asking himself: "Did I do this and that correctly?"'

'He does not like it when we disagree about something, if I say, "yes" and he says "no". It simply makes him feel bad.'

When you talk to Paul today, he does not disagree fundamentally with how she sees him. It was a long journey up to this point and she was with him every step of the way – but first there was a critical event.

After the dominee strong-armed them into wedlock, Paul asked his mother if Smokie could come and live with him in George. For she was still looking after the little war orphan he stuffed into her arms when he returned home from the Border.

Lynette immediately realised that the dog was important to Paul, but because of his silence about Smokeshell, she did not understand why.

'Smokie was a little mongrel, a true pavement special. He was a bit of everything, maybe he even had some Cuban blood! But the dog only had eyes for Paul. The two of them had a special bond and I suppose I may have been a touch jealous of that. But Smokie was also a wanderer and one day he just disappeared.'

Paul picks up the story: 'At times Smokie would slip out the front door and disappear. Sometimes he would just turn up again after two or three days. Or somebody would phone from wherever in George and say, "Paul, your dog is over here," and I would go pick him up.'

One Friday afternoon in 1996, Smokie went wandering again. 'On the Saturday afternoon I phoned the SPCA and described Smokie and they said, ja, he's with them but I can only go pick him up that Monday.'

But Smokie, who survived the battle of Smokeshell in a Swapo bunker, had run out of luck. He had been set upon by feral dogs before being rescued by a stranger and taken to the SPCA.

'When I arrived at the SPCA on Monday he was virtually torn to bits. I took him to a vet, old Dr Deacon, but he just shook his head and said, "No, the dog is not going to make it." So I said okay, the dog's very old, in that case just put him down.'

Paul was shattered by the brutal end of the dog he saved at Smokeshell 15 years earlier.

'When I left the vet's office, I drove straight to a liquor store and bought a bottle of brandy. By the time Lynette got home I was drunk and the hi-fi was playing at full blast. She immediately saw that something was wrong.'

Lynette recalls that day vividly.

'I stopped in the driveway and heard the music blasting from the stereo. It was very strange behaviour; usually he would turn up the music a bit on a Friday after work. I walked into the house and found the kids watching TV in the living room and they said, "Shhh, mom … Pollie is in the study and he's very sad."'

'Pollie' was how Lynette's children from her first marriage fondly addressed Paul. 'I wondered what the hell happened. Then I saw him sitting at his desk with a picture of Smokie and all his Smokeshell stuff. A bottle of brandy and a glass, no Coke as I recall. He was devastated.'

After five years of marriage, he finally opened up to her about what he had seen and experienced in Angola, and she realised the extent of the emotional wounds he had kept hidden. 'So I started pressing him to go and see a psychiatrist.'

Paul is deeply grateful to Lynette for the way she handled that situation: 'She did not withdraw. She bathed the kids, put them to bed and then we talked and talked. And she basically just accepted things – and me.'

But it was just the start of his long and rough road to healing.

When things went wrong in his previous marriages he went for couples counselling. 'But it was all, "This is what a man should do, this is what a woman should do" … They never dug any deeper than that,' Lynette reflects.

Now they set out to find the right psychologist to dig deep, but it proved to be no easy thing.

She suggested a psychologist in George who had some training in working with war veterans. But it seemed that Paul did not want to accept this man's authority, so they called it a day after a number of sessions.

Still, Lynette gained some valuable insights from some of the sessions she attended: 'He told us certain triggers made Paul withdraw. Like the smell of diesel, large fires, people who argue, people who say it's not good enough, it's your fault.'

Lynette and Paul Louw in their living room in George.

Paul elaborates: 'Lynette and I went to several shrinks. There was the guy in George who styled himself as a debriefing specialist. I had three sessions with him, but it was all about him wanting to calm you to a sort of trance-like state ... and then you were supposed to talk about everything that troubled you.'

They kept trying, but their personal relationship was starting to suffer. 'We were not growing as a couple, there were obstructions and I did not know why,' Lynette says. 'I would phone my sister and tell her I did not know what to do anymore. And then her husband would say: "It's the fucking war! It's Angola, that's why Paul can't settle." And I would think, really? But he was right.'

When they finally found the right person to help Paul, it was due to their relationship issues rather than his war trauma: 'There was this woman who styled herself as a marriage counsellor, but she had psychological expertise. From her I learned your marriage is like two paths running side by side. Sometimes, when something happens, one path veers away from the other.'

Like when he withdrew because of some trigger or another, Paul realised.

'But when you sort out the problem, your path swings back to your partner's again – as long as you do not allow it to grow too far apart.

'Lynette grasped this. So when I tried to withdraw again, she simply would not let me. Like the day I just started packing my bags and she walked into the room and said, "Where are you going?" And I said I'm leaving, I'm going to get into my car and drive away. So she took another bag and started packing and said, "Then I'm coming with you." That's how Lynette was.'

As usual, Lynette has a more pragmatic view of why this marriage counsellor was the right match: 'She was this little bundle of a person and she would just gently scold him when he was being difficult. And because she was this tiny woman, he felt safe when she told him who he was and why. She taught us a lot about trauma and how it worked.'

Through all this emotional trauma, Lynette stuck with Paul, even when he briefly sought recognition elsewhere. She never again allowed him to wrestle his demons alone. 'When we have a problem, we name it and then we go sit down and talk about the solution.'

Then, one day in 2008, Paul received an unexpected phone call.

The voice on the other end of the line belonged to HP Ferreira, his Ratel driver, who had been so gravely wounded that he was mistakenly reported as dead. Back then, he came to grief as he instinctively tried to follow Paul on the battlefield. And now it was

HP who reached out to Paul to join other Smokeshell veterans for a reunion in Bloemfontein. Paul was reluctant, 'but he said it would mean a lot to him. And HP can be quite convincing!'

Unbeknown to HP, he had an ally in Lynette. For the woman with the healing hands of a physiotherapist and the insights of a psychologist understood that this would be the next big step on Paul's road to inner peace.

When Paul started ducking and diving, she simply said: 'You're going, and I'm going with you. We're going to Bloemfontein and we'll take it from there. And so he started getting used to the idea and we went. That first time was such an emotional happening, they were all so happy to see Paul.'

After 28 years the dam wall finally broke, Paul agrees.

'When Lynette and I got out of the car at 1 SAI and saw those guys standing there … Jeez, that was a turning point. I realised I was not the only one who mistakenly clung to the "cowboys don't cry" thing for so many years.'

Cowboys don't cry … that tough-guy act hammered into so many South African men from a tender young age. Real men never show they're hurting inside, they just carry on. But on that day in Bloemfontein, Paul, HP, Marco and the others cried and talked and then cried some more.

Cassie Schoeman, one of Paul's father figures, was also there.

'I always had the highest respect for Oom Cassie as a military leader. And there he was, crying like a child. And what of it? It did not make him a lesser or weaker man; it made him a better man in my eyes. A leader who shows his emotions, and that is important.'

That weekend they worked through their feelings as a group like never before. Safe in the knowledge that they were sharing with people who had been through what they had, who understood and did not judge. Guys who were also young and scared back then.

'Back in George, after that weekend, Lynette told me: "You're a different human being, you're not the same as before. You're open to arguments and potential conflict. You don't just turn away from it. You get involved in a positive way that is acceptable to others."'

The Bloemfontein gathering on 10 June became an institution for Smokeshell veterans, as did the larger gathering for all 61 Mech veterans in Johannesburg in August. Paul attended both on a regular basis. As a result, his need for formal counselling melted away, Lynette believes, 'because talking to other veterans was therapeutic'.

Paul is on the same page: 'In all honesty, I feel very fortunate to be able to talk about these things. People have different ways of dealing with trauma. Some require medication, others go back to the bush and stay there. I say just open up. What are you going to lose? If some people call you crazy for doing so, what about it? They don't know you. Everybody in this world is a little bit crazy, nobody is completely sane.

'Everybody should talk about this kind of stuff. Forget the macho business. Life is too short to suppress all these emotions and carry the burden by yourself. For me, the solution is to talk about it.'

And talk he did. Gert Minnaar, a founding member of 61 MVA, put the TV journalist Ruda Landman on Paul's trail. In 2010, he appeared on her programme about trauma, with HP and Marco. As a result, family members of other troubled veterans started approaching Paul for advice and help.

'You know, even if I could help only one person, it would be well worth it,' he says.

And sometimes he was indeed able to get somebody started on the road to healing with a long telephone call or personal visit, or by helping a family member to find closure. Like the day in 2010 when his golfing partner said, shortly after tee off: 'You know, there's a Tannie Kruger who desperately wants to talk to you ...'

She was none other than the mother of Corporal Paul Kruger, the gymkhana Springbok who died at Smokeshell after he could not get leave to ride in an international tournament in South Africa. 'She was from Grahamstown or somewhere in the Eastern Cape and still devastated by the death of her son. When Louis Harmse and the chaplain turned up at her house back then to speak with her, she chased them away, withdrew from her church and community and basically became a hermit.'

But then she saw Paul on Ruda's programme and reached out to him through his golfing partner, Johan, who used to live in the same town as the Kruger family: 'Johan gave me her phone number and we had a long conversation. At the end of it she forgave everybody for the heartache of living without her son and returned to the fold of her church congregation. She even sent me a photograph of Paul's grave. So it just goes to show, if you can help even one person by talking, well then, you've helped that one person.'

Thanks to Marco, he was able to talk to the deceased Rob de Vito's mother and sister and meet an uncle of Piet Joubert. But so many others, including Smokeshell veterans, continue to withdraw to this day. Some are unable to maintain relationships or hold down jobs: 'There are guys who I want to go look up again.'

Other parts of his life did not stand still. He got a master's degree in city planning and, as second-in-command of the Knysna Commando, he became deeply involved in rural safety and fighting mountain fires (he's a military man at heart, Lynette says). It seems that Paul did indeed become the man his father was.

How does Smokeshell affect him more than 40 years later?

'Firstly, it taught me to respect human life. In the later stage of my life it softened me and made me realise your life can change in the blink of an eye, and it upsets me when others don't see that.

'I have come to deeply resent those arrogant people who show contempt for the lives of others. Whether it's people who handle firearms or vehicles recklessly, or city planners who force through decisions that will negatively affect communities and then say, "Man, it doesn't matter, people will adapt."'

But Smokeshell also taught him to carry on – regardless of how bad things are.

'In spite of everything, we came out of the army stronger because of our training and because we learned to persevere. It made us into adults.'

To open up about the war after 28 years of silence also taught him a valuable new skill: 'It took me that long to learn to argue something through with somebody until you reach a solution that you're both happy with.

'When we were young, we took part in military operations because we had to. When you received an order, you carried it out and that was that. That is how you were raised and how you were trained.

'When you're young you think you can run through walls. But there are smarter ways to get to the other side of walls. I learned to think about situations and to look for solutions that will prevent conflict and drama, to shape and pursue reasonable arguments ... These are instincts I did not always have.

'Right up to 2008 I did not want to talk about Smokeshell at all because I felt responsible for the deaths of 12 people. Only when I started talking to the other guys did I realise, no, they do not think I was responsible … Well, maybe there are some who think so, but those I talked to said: "No Paul, it's not like that. We were there, this is what happened, and you were not responsible."'

For 28 years he interrogated himself relentlessly: 'I said to myself thousands of times, if only I did this, that would not have happened. But opening up in 2008 helped me to feel less guilty. What happened, happened. Our losses could have been even greater.'

His bonds with his blood brothers are stronger than ever and for that, above all else, he is grateful: 'It's of overwhelming importance to me.'

A footnote from Lynette: when she accompanied him to that first informal Bloemfontein gathering in 2008, she chose not to be present during the long and emotional talks between the men. Instead, she was there for him when he returned to their guest house in the evening.

But in 2020 the annual gathering of hundreds of 61 Mech veterans and their families in Johannesburg was not possible owing to the Covid-19 pandemic. The alternative was much smaller regional gatherings all over the country, wherever veterans lived.

Paul led the gathering in the Southern Cape and for the first time she heard him opening up to other veterans at first hand. Lynette recalls: 'He told them exactly what went wrong, why they were in the wrong place at the wrong time, but he did not blame anyone. He spoke of the lack of support, counselling and therapy by the defence force. But he never said the army was bad, he never blamed the army for what he went through. He does not have this hatred for the army like some guys do.

'My mother-in-law and my sister-in-law were also there and

Blood brothers at a Smokeshell gathering in Bloemfontein, 2017.
From left: Peter Brent, Marco Caforio, Paul Louw and HP Ferreira.

together we heard it all for the first time. It seemed as if Paul really had closure. He's one of the lucky people who got out of Smokeshell in one piece. And, after all these years, every time he returns from a 61 Mech reunion, he seems to have even more peace.'

As Paul himself puts it: 'To talk is how I medicate.'

And then he got another unexpected telephone call. This time it was his former unit commander, the now retired General Johann Dippenaar. And he heard him say the astonishing words: 'Are you ready to go back to the Angolan bush ... back to Smokeshell?'

12

OTHER PATHS TO HEALING: GARETH AND JAN

They were two of the lucky members of Paul Louw's Platoon 1, emerging from hell without wounds of the visible kind.

Gareth, the medic and philosopher who always poured his heart out on paper, and Jan, the driver who instinctively knew that, because of his dyslexia, he had to find his own way through life if he wanted to be successful. Two very different guys thrown together by the army in the same section and therefore in the same Ratel – 21B, the only one in their platoon not chewed up by enemy anti-aircraft fire. Two survivors still in Angola after their dead and wounded buddies were choppered away.

They lacked physical wounds, but no young mind could be left untouched by what they had just seen and experienced. Adrenaline and terror gave way to exhaustion, followed by shock, anger and sorrow. Gareth, who fought so hard to keep his injured friends alive, battled to make sense of it all. For the less eloquent Jan, it was simply 'very bad'.

Both wanted to get the hell away from that place after the fighting stopped, but the job was not done. The trenches, bunkers and bodies had to be searched for documents, personal letters, pictures – any scrap of information that could be of use to the intelligence effort. A huge quantity of captured arms, ammunition and equipment had to be gathered, sorted and loaded into choppers and vehicles to be hauled back south. Then there was the never-ending routine of cleaning and maintaining everything from personal weapons to Ratels so that they were combat-ready. There were foot patrols of the surrounding area under the hot sun by day and sentry duty during the freezing nights.

One night, the silence was shattered by the hollow thump of Swapo mortars and the crackling of AK-47 fire as the South African laager was attacked. Gareth dived under a Ratel with sandbags stacked between the big wheels for extra protection, 'but the 'bats soon drove them off'. (These were the parabats who could not be choppered in for the attack on Smokeshell. They arrived the next day in Buffel troop carriers and were deployed in a defensive perimeter around the 61 Mech laager.)

As always, the rumour mill was grinding away. 'We're going to attack again,' followed shortly by 'No, we're not.' 'We're going to push further north, deeper into Angola.' 'Okay, no, we're not.' Every fresh rumour put them on edge; every new denial made them gatvol.

About a week after the attack their provisions were running low, Jan recalls, 'so we were ordered to escort a logistical convoy back across the border to pick up diesel, food and whatever.'

So, with Jan behind the wheel of the Ratel and Gareth and the rest of the section in the back, they trundled back to Ondangwa on the South West African side. And for the first time in two weeks they enjoyed luxuries like warm showers, cold beer, fresh food prepared in a kitchen and a video night. For Gareth, simply to crawl into his sleeping bag without fearing attack was fantastic.

All too soon, they were on their way back to the combat group laagered near Smokeshell. On the way, an Eland armoured car broke down, and much to Jan's chagrin he had to tow 'that bloody little Noddy car' with his Ratel the rest of the way. But then, while rounding a corner, the Eland ran off the sandy track and hit a tree. It was now too damaged for Jan to tow.

And there was more bad news for Jan, Gareth and their buddies. They were still 20 km from the 61 Mech laager – a long way to go over that kind of terrain. The logistical convoy had to push on but somebody had to stay behind to guard the wrecked Eland until a recovery team could be sent. Guess who?

'"We're coming back for you now-now," the sergeant said as they started up … but we just knew we were not going to see him again,' Jan recalls. So they started preparing for whatever the hell was going to happen next. With sandbags they turned the Ratel into a small fortified position. The 20 mil cannon and the Browning machine gun were loaded and ready to go, as were the armoured car's big 90 mil cannon and Browning.

Jan's gut feel was spot-on. For as darkness cloaked the bush there was still no sign of the cavalry. It would be a long and bitterly cold night. Gareth sums up their situation: 'There we were, just the 12 of us, in the middle of the Angolan bush with Swapo somewhere out there. We had to be absolutely quiet, no fires or lights.'

For Jan, the night was fraught with danger.

'We paired up with a buddy on guard duty or when trying to sleep. I was so scared that night, you start seeing things everywhere. Something stirs and you stare and stare at that spot and eventually a blerrie cow walks out of the bush.'

The night seemed to last forever. Finally, with the sun already arcing over the bush, they heard the whining roar of Ratel engines approaching. Their relief was boundless.

More long days of foot patrols and maintenance followed. And more rumours and boredom.

Finally, the combat group left Angola and returned to Omuthiya. There was a parade in Tsumeb's main street, with the old copper-mine shaft at one end and the German colonial church at the other. The women of the town served the troops tea and cakes.

Gareth was immensely relieved to be back in Omuthiya. There was the heartache of all the empty places in Platoon 1's tents but also the joy of once again seeing Paul Louw, Marco Caforio and the others who had been wounded.

There were bittersweet moments during their last weeks 'on the Border'. They did vehicle patrols in the Etosha area and the farm folk were as hospitable as before. The troops were spoilt with homemade food and acts of kindness.

There was a night when Jan sat in a sunken hide overlooking a waterhole. The full moon turned night into day: 'Then the elephants came to drink out of the bush behind me and they walk over the concrete roof of the hide and through the viewing slit you see their great feet just in front of your face, so big but silent as ghosts. It was such a magical feeling.'

But there was also the day when they arrived at a farm where Platoon 1 had patrolled and camped before they ever heard of a place called Smokeshell: 'The farmer and his wife recognised us from before and asked why there were so few of us this time … So we told them what happened. That tannie just could not stop crying.'

Finally, they left the base under the camelthorn trees to walk up the tail ramp of a Flossie at Grootfontein for the flight back to the

Gareth Rutherford next to the wreck of Paul Louw's Ratel 21, loaded onto a tiffie truck.

Gareth Rutherford (right) and a mate safely back at Omuthiya after Smokeshell.

States. It was time to return to civvy street and carry on with their lives as best they could.

Their future paths would be very different.

GARETH RUTHERFORD

At his dining room table in picturesque and pastoral Swellendam, the former ops medic turns the yellowed pages of his war diary.

Occasionally, Gareth pauses to read his thoughts from so long ago with dramatic emphasis. Close your eyes and you could be listening to a radio serial. But then he turns to the motivational card Dippenaar gave his troops on the morning of the attack and you know it was all too real.

Gareth's copy, pasted into the diary, is smudged with the blood of some of the buddies he tried to save four decades ago. And, all along the edges, surrounding 61 Mech's lightning bolt and the printed words of encouragement, he penned the names of the dead in blue ink. But one name he crossed out later – that of HP, who was listed as dead but who survived.

For the greatest part of his life after Smokeshell, this tall, slim man carried a great burden of guilt: 'It took me 30 years to realise that it was not my doing that they died. It was time that took them away, they were bleeding inside.'

How he finally came to that conclusion is yet another dramatic story.

Gareth's feelings of guilt were deepened when he was awarded South Africa's highest honour for bravery. He vividly remembers the day he first heard that he was to be singled out in this manner.

When Bravo Company returned from the Border, they passed the last few weeks of their national service at Lohatla, a vast expanse of Karoo veld where live battle exercises up to regimental

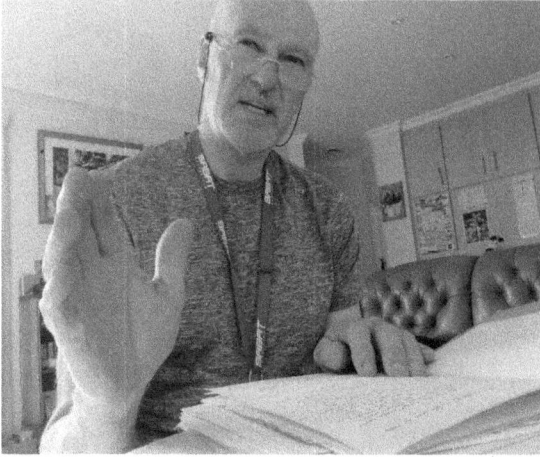

Decades after Smokeshell, Gareth Rutherford
consults his war diary once more.

level could be conducted. There, Gareth the medic was pushed
into service as a field cook: 'I loved cooking, my mom taught me
as a boy and I always cooked with passion.'

He was manning the hotboxes (army food containers) when
the company was told to fall in: 'Captain Harmse spoke to us,
complimenting us for our conduct during Operation Smokeshell
for the first time. And then, completely out of the blue, I heard
him say: "The Honoris Crux has been awarded to Lance Corporal
Rutherford."

'I looked to my left and right down the rank and smiled, because
I thought he was joking. We then waited, thinking more names
would be read out, but there was none.' (The Honoris Crux was
also awarded to Peter Brent, who had helped Gareth to comfort
the wounded on the battlefield, but he refused it. Brent, who
emigrated to Britain after the war, said he would accept the medal
only if it was awarded to the whole of Platoon 1.)

Gareth Rutherford receives the Honoris Crux for bravery from Prime Minister PW Botha.

Gareth did not know how to feel: 'I was happy, astonished, confused and proud, all at the same time. I took one step forward, the captain shook my hand and a few of the guys clapped weakly.'

He had no idea why he had been singled out for this honour, as no citation was read out during the brief announcement: 'Then the whole company just fell out and got into their vehicles … A few guys said, "Well done," but there was no cheering. It was all very muted.'

It was late afternoon and the day's training was over, so Gareth stacked the empty hotboxes on the kitchen truck. Then he decided to run the five kilometres back to camp: 'I wanted to think. But my brain was in a turmoil and I missed the track that turned off to our tents. Pretty soon I was lost but I just kept running.'

As his arms and legs pumped away it dawned on him that the medal was for assisting his dying buddies in the bush. And his next thought was: 'Why was I the one who lived?'

PART A. - RECOMMENDATIONS

1. No. 75245985 BG .... Rank: Lance Corporal ... Full names and
   military post-nominal titles ..... Gareth Timothy Rutherford ....
Unit .... South African Infantry Battalion ....
Corps ... South African Infantry Corps.

Action for which commended: During the attack on Smokeshell in June 1980.
Lance Corporal Rutherford gave medical assistance to his section and
other members of the platoon, three of whom were still alive and four
members having died of wounds.

He had to move approximately 40 metres from his own vehicle to where the
injured were and whilst doing this he had to fight the enemy, who were
hidden in the trees and bushes between himself and the injured.   When he
reached the injured, who were still under enemy fire, he immediately com-
menced giving them medical assistance.

Lance Corporal Rutherford then returned to his vehicle, whilst still under
enemy fire, to salvage his medical kit, so that he could continue to render
first aid. He applied intravenous drips to the wounded in spite of the
fact that he knew two of the seriously wounded, Riflemen Warrener and Madden,
would not survive. He then proceeded to encourage the survivors whilst
the battle was still raging about him.

It is recommended that the Honoris Crux be awarded to Lance Corporal
Rutherford for his act of bravery in leaving his vehicle, where he was
sheltered from enemy fire, and fighting his way through the enemy to render
medical assistance to his comrades, thus saving their lives and boosting
their morale.

The citation for Gareth's medal. Only decades after the battle would he
hear that it was written by Paul Louw.

That question would haunt him for many years.

He was still running aimlessly when darkness started to fall: 'I
stumbled upon a group of Citizen Force guys and they gave me
a beer. I told them what just happened and they, total strangers,
cheered me as if I was one of their own. They were so kind.'

They drove him to his own camp, about eight kilometres back

down the dirt road, but Gareth recalls little of the ride: 'I was feeling morose and depressed. I was confused because I was being rewarded while so many of my buddies, the real heroes, were dead.'

The award ceremony took place in Bloemfontein in 1981, the year after he left the army. The medal was pinned to Gareth's uniform tunic by Prime Minister PW Botha. His proud parents were flown to the Free State capital, put up in a hotel and treated as special guests during the award ceremony and reception: 'They met PW, Magnus Malan and all the other big brass. But for me, just an ordinary lance corporal, it was all very scary. I felt unworthy and kept thinking of the families of the dead.'

Because you never forget the smell of blood or the faces of the dying. They revisit you in your nightmares and you hear their last words again and again. As Gareth got on with his life he carried those memories with him, as did so many others of his generation.

Eventually, he too would turn a corner. Ironically, it took another bloody and destructive conflict for this to come about.

On 11 September 2001, members of the terror group al-Qaeda hijacked four airliners and flew them into the World Trade Center in New York and the Pentagon in Washington, DC. They were like missiles stuffed with people. The carnage was horrific and the world was plunged into a new kind of war.

On March 2003, a vengeful US and a coalition of allies invaded Iraq, which the US government controversially linked to the events of 9/11. The Iraqi dictator, Saddam Hussein, was deposed and the Americans vowed to rebuild the country.

Gareth, by then experienced in the field of civil engineering, was one of many South Africans who grasped the opportunity to do contract work in Iraq. The money was good but the country was still pretty much a war zone – even though the Americans had declared themselves the victors. 'Iraq was just crazy, it was so dangerous,' Gareth says today. 'I'm amazed that I'm still alive.'

But he took risks and worked hard. After five years, he was in charge of all logistics and operations for a British company in Iraq: 'When others chose to get the hell out of that country, I stayed. Like everybody else, I was going around with bags full of cash to pay for stuff. That's how it worked over there.'

He prided himself that he could make any deal or project work, no matter how tough or dangerous it was. Reckless and arrogant, a regular cowboy but efficient, is how he describes himself in that time and place: 'My reputation was on the line, as was that of my British employer.'

But, in the process, he trod on the toes of powerful and corrupt role players, he believes. Because ten years in a Middle Eastern prison was never part of the game plan.

It was in 2008 when everything went nuts. At the time, he was regularly ferrying materials between the Iraqi city of Basra and the neighbouring country of Kuwait, Gareth explains.

'One day a business contact phoned and asked me to go pick up cement samples across the border in Kuwait … I agreed because we were already tied up in contracts worth millions with this guy's company.'

Before he set off to collect the samples, he loaded a cargo of old run-flat tyres that he needed repaired. But when he arrived at the workshop like so many times before, the police were waiting for him … and they found hashish stuffed inside the tyres.

Gareth maintains his innocence to this day. 'I was set up, I was framed.' But a Kuwaiti court decided differently and he was sentenced to life in prison for smuggling narcotics.

'I was made a scapegoat by those who wanted to get rid of a

competitor who was way too successful. As a result, the British company I worked for had to pull out of Iraq entirely.'

During his years in a desert prison, Gareth found ways to record his emotions – just as he did during the Border War – and he's working with a ghost writer to get his recollections published. In short, he once again found himself in a very dark place: 'You can never know what it's like if you haven't been there yourself … right at the bottom of the pit with nothing.'

His time in prison cost him his marriage and wrecked his relationship with his son. But gradually, he started gleaning positives from his surroundings: 'There were so many ordinary people in prison, poor folk who had absolutely nothing. But they were so unbelievably kind to me. They became wonderful friends who treated me with sympathy and understanding.'

His pleas for his case to be reviewed fell on deaf ears. 'But eventually the local British embassy started looking after me. They brought me basic necessities like toiletries and my situation started improving. Eventually I was the only one with a bed while my cellmates slept on the floor … and it made me feel guilty, just like getting the medal for Smokeshell.'

And in time his social status grew. He became a sort of mentor and adviser to other prisoners, many of whom were not literate. As he had learned to read and write Arabic during his years working in Iraq, he recited the Quran 'like a parrot' with other inmates while praying fervently to his own God. Gareth also made himself useful to the prison authorities as he had the skills to fix air-conditioning units and other appliances.

Like any prison *ouman*, he got hold of forbidden technology to communicate with the outside world from his cell. Among those who followed Gareth's online updates was another 61 Mech veteran – Dawid Lotter, who participated in military operations in Angola and rose to the rank of major before leaving the SADF. After returning to civilian life, Dawid published several books and volumes of poetry about the war and its impact on soldiers.

Dawid believed in Gareth's innocence and could not ignore the plight of a fellow veteran so far from home. He started a petition to raise public awareness and call for Gareth's release. But his freedom would not be gained overnight.

In his cell in the faraway desert state, Gareth wrote prolifically. The British embassy collected his writings and sent them off to his mom in Kalk Bay. Sadly, she fell ill and died while he was behind bars. Gareth was heartbroken, and it was his fellow inmates – 'simple, wonderful people' – who consoled him in his grief.

If there was one thing he had plenty of, it was time. Time to reflect on that bloody day in the bush, to think of the men he could not save, despite his best efforts, and the medal that made him feel guilty. And finally, in the most unlikely place and circumstance, he started to find his peace.

In November 2018, he was released, 'thanks to Dawid Lotter who made such a noise with his petition', and flew home. The community of Kalk Bay turned out to welcome him like a lost son and returning hero. In the spirit of the popular song, yellow ribbons were symbolically tied around the trees lining the streets. A huge yellow banner read 'Welcome home Gareth' and media interviews followed.

As the shadow of the Langeberge lengthens over Swellendam, he reads again – this time from his prison diary. For on the eve of his release he reflected on Smokeshell one more time and wrote: 'I realised that I did all the right things as I was trained to do. That senior officer who I yelled at because the choppers were not coming also saw that I did everything I could. There, among all those flying bullets, I kept my head and for that I thank my medical instructor, Dr James Gibson. All the medical procedures I performed that day were correct.'

His diary also reflects his belief that any credit due was not his alone: 'I have since read the stories of others who were also there, the guys in our section and our platoon and our company. It is thanks to all of them that I am still alive today. I would be dead if it were not for them. It was all one great team effort.'

The entry ends: 'It took me years to discover that I did nothing that I should be ashamed of. Today I am proud, I do not feel ashamed or guilty anymore. I am proud that I did what I was trained to do, and that I did it well.'

Spoken as a truly free man at last.

But there is one last footnote here. Quite recently, Paul Louw revealed to Gareth it was he – and not that unknown senior officer he yelled at on the battlefield – who wrote the citation for Gareth's medal.

JAN HOEVERS

Because of Jan's dyslexia, reading and writing was a challenge, so dabbling in amateur psychology was definitely not a thing for him. But like so often in his young life, Jan would follow his instincts.

The army taught them many things, he explains today. But never how to deal with what they went through in Angola: 'And for me that was the worst. That day when we klaared out in Bloem … all the other platoons were at full strength. But even with our wounded back, Platoon 1 numbered only 25 or so. That's a hell of a difference from 44.'

'Then the last order was shouted: "UITKLAAR!" And that was that. They might as well have told us to fuck off, we're done with you now. I always imagined we would throw our berets into the air and cheer, like you see in the movies. Hugs and handshakes and all that. But no, all the guys just walked away in silence with their heads down.

'I so looked forward to klaaring out, but at that moment all I could think was: "What the fuck now?" I had my old railways job to go back to, but what do I do with all this stuff in my head? Nobody said they were sorry for what happened to us. Those words you never heard in the army.'

But unlike so many others who bottled up everything, Jan's gut would tell him how to go about DIY therapy. He needed no telling that the whole macho thing was nonsense.

After leaving the army, he spent a week with his parents, who now lived in Centurion, before returning to his job as an assistant train driver. But Jan wanted nothing more to do with the army and those compulsory Citizen Force camps. As his job was still classified as a key position, he duly filed for exemption every time he received call-up papers.

After two-and-a-half years, with enough time accrued on the railways to exempt him from further call-ups, he resigned again. Jan was still convinced he had to be his own boss to succeed in life. It would prove to be a rough road, but he never feared failure.

'I used all my savings to buy a video shop in Capital Park, in Pretoria. The first video I ever watched was in my own shop, that's how little I knew about the business! It took me less than three years to go bust. So I just tried something new, and when that failed something else again ... and so on.'

For years he was the proverbial rolling stone: 'I lived in youth hostels, sometimes I rented cheap hotel rooms or lodgings. Or stayed on somebody's smallholding or with friends. Everything I owned I could pack into my car, and the mattress I tied onto the roof.'

One thing, however, he did with dogged consistency. Whenever he got half a chance, he talked of what he had seen and done in Angola. Strangers, friends, it made no difference. Whenever he could, he instinctively unburdened. 'Ja, most people actually listened,' he says with wry humour. 'I suppose they did not hear that kind of stuff every day.'

And he could not care less whether people believed him or not: 'I just wanted to get it all out of me. I remember the day I was waiting in a long line at a Spar or something … an old man was standing behind me and I just turned around and started telling him about the army.

'The line moved forward and eventually my stuff and his was cashed up but I never stopped talking. So I just took his shopping bags and carried it to his car but I never stopped talking. Eventually I noticed the old man was crying … so I loaded his shopping into his car and left him alone.'

Today, he believes all that talking made it easier to readapt to civvy life: 'I think the longer you clam up, the harder it gets to open up. You know, my dad was in World War II and he never wanted to talk about it. A lot of guys don't want to talk about it, but fortunately I never had that guy thing.

'The day we klaared out I realised I was carrying around a lot of sadness. Our half a platoon, the sadness on everybody's faces … That's baggage, right? But the more you talk about it, the easier it gets to haul.

'If only the army gave us some basic guidance a week or

Jan Hoevers, builder king of Great Brak River.

Jan and his wife, Ricky, on their new boat.

two before we klaared out. You know, like, "Tell your story to somebody whether that person believes you or not. And then tell it to the next guy, and the next. Four, five times a day. And if they don't believe you, remember you were there; they were not. Telling your story makes you stronger, not weaker."'

Jan sucks on his pipe for a moment before he rounds off his thoughts.

'I have a lot of respect for the army. They trained us well, taught us the importance of maintaining and looking after equipment, and that you never leave a buddy behind. The one bad thing is that they neglected mental health. There was zip, nothing. Many guys may have been better off today if only the army gave us some guidance on how to heal.'

Eventually, his dogged dream to be his own man led him to the picturesque town of Great Brak River, just up the coast from Mossel Bay, about 25 years ago. There he parked his bakkie and tools at the town entrance with a sign advertising his services as a builder. Of anything, big or small. Jan, a man with skilful hands and a lot of natural business acumen, soon prospered.

The rolling stone came to a halt and gathered a considerable amount of moss. On a high bluff overlooking the river and estuary, Jan built himself a replica of a medieval castle, complete with ramparts and turrets. 'So people can see who the king of the builders in Grootbrak is. You have to show off a bit, you know,' he grins.

There's an inner courtyard with water features and sculptures, and the interior of his swanky abode could grace the pages of a glossy magazine. Yes, he hired a professional interior designer to do the decor – and then he married her. Ricky is now the queen of Jan's castle.

The man who drove a train and a Ratel also became a mariner. He learned to sail, became a qualified skipper and bought a yacht: 'Ag, I like new projects and doing different things, you know. I like to be busy, there's always something new.'

Over the years he bumped into a fellow Smokeshell veteran here and there. He also attended one of those early gatherings in Bloemfontein but never felt the need to be a regular.

'I'm on a Smokeshell WhatsApp group. Some guys chat in the group every day, sometimes just to say good morning and share good wishes. I respect that. I read all the messages every day and sometimes I'll post a joke.'

He also calls a couple of guys on a regular basis. Mostly, he appreciates the fact that safe spaces – physical or on social media – exist where the Smokeshell generation can express themselves freely. 'It's so important ... When I read the messages, I can see that some guys are still searching for peace.'

Personally, he feels 'as free as a bird because I talked and got it all out of me. It was a fluke that I did the right thing, nobody told me to do it. Afterwards I thought, maybe I'm not as dumb as I look!'

As our interview winds down I ask Jan if there's anything else he'd like to say. 'No, I've finished spinning my story now,' he answers in his slow Afrikaans drawl.

And you know that's that.

PART 3

BACK TO THE KILLING FIELD

13
THE QUEST

One day in 1981, Johann Dippenaar handed over command of
61 Mech and took his leave of the base he had built under the
camelthorn trees of Ovamboland. In time, a plinth and needle
of dark grey marble would be erected in the heart of Omuthiya.
On this memorial the names of the 13 men who paid the highest
price for 61 Mech's first cross-border operational success would be
carved, as well as those of the casualties that would follow.

In time, many more names would be carved on that needle.

Dippenaar was not bound for civvy street, however. From 61
Mech he moved on to the next chapter of a long and distinguished
military career in which he would rise to the rank of general. But
he never forgot the men – living or dead – he led at Smokeshell.

In 2005, with the Border War long over, 61 Mech was disbanded.
Two former national service lieutenants, Gert Minnaar and Ariël
Hugo, were determined that all the glory and sacrifice would
not be forgotten. And they wanted to create a safe space for the
thousands of former unit members.

During a small but significant meeting held in Caledon in 2007,
the foundation was laid for a 61 Mech veterans' organisation.
It would be a place where everyone could rub shoulders on an
equal footing, regardless of their rank or role when they still wore

browns. The response was heartening and, in 2008, Dippenaar was elected as the first chairman. As always, he got things done.

He was among those who attended the Smokeshell reunions in Bloemfontein from the outset. And he was a driving force behind the big annual 61 Mech commemoration day at the Johannesburg war museum (formally the Ditsong National Museum of Military History). But it was a 61 Mech veterans' tour of the old Angolan battlefields (one of several over the years) that lit a fire in him.

Dippenaar flew in for the highlight of the 2018 tour: the memorial service at the notorious bridge near Cuito Cuanavale. But the rest of the sizeable tour group drove in convoy to every place where 61 Mech fought – except Smokeshell, for nobody knew exactly where it was. Among those in the convoy who made an unsuccessful attempt to find it were Marco Caforio, Kelvin Luke and Mike Beyl. It was as if the bush itself had swallowed the old Swapo trenches and gun positions.

Dippenaar, who was back home in Pretoria by then, was deeply moved when he heard how Marco and the others tried to find the place where they fought and suffered so long ago: 'There and then, at the age of 75, I vowed that I would rediscover the exact location of Smokeshell before I kick the bucket.'

His plan was simple: to search until he found it, at his own cost, and alone if needs be. And then to take his men back there to erect a memorial for the fallen.

Easy it would not be, for even in 1980 there were no geographical or man-made landmarks. Only the bush. And GPS navigation did not exist. This, however, did not deter Dippenaar. Did he not spend days poring over the maps constructed from scraps of intelligence to plan the attack? And did he not direct the construction of scale models of the targets and drill every little detail into the minds of his officers and NCOs?

So, decades later, he sat down in his Pretoria home and started redrawing the maps. And by January 2020 he was ready go to Angola and start the physical search: 'I believed if I could find the objective way back then, I would find it again all these years later.'

The next step was to activate the vast and resourceful network of 61 Mech veterans.

'I asked Thys Rall, who was a member of my team way back then, to fly me up to Ondangwa in Namibia. (Thys, a former second-in-command of 61 Mech, had started a small air charter service based in Windhoek after he left the military.)

At Ondangwa, Dippenaar was met by two other men who knew how to get things done. One was Martin Bremer, a former 61 Mech lieutenant on the armour side of things who was awarded the Honoris Crux for bravery during Operation Moduler: 'I did not know Bremer at all, but what a gem of a man. He just walked up to me and said: "I'm taking you there."' (Bremer was also the man who, in 2018, led a small group of veterans to find the wrecked Ratel of their friend Mielie Meiring, who died in 61 Mech's last battle in Angola, against a huge Cuban force, in 1988.[2])

'So I climbed into his 4x4 only to discover this guy Stefan sitting there. [Stefan van Wyk, yet another South African military veteran, chose to settle in Angola in civilian life.] And jissie, what stars these two men turned out to be.'

The trio crossed into Angola – legally, via a border post, this time – then reconnected with the original approach route. In the

2 The search for Mielie's Ratel is described in my book *Die Brug: Na die Hel en Terug in Angola*.

One of the old gun positions on the Smokeshell battlefield today.

Some of the old trenches, almost reclaimed by dirt and leaves.

front passenger seat, Dippenaar studied his hand-drawn map and gave directions to Martin, who was behind the wheel. He recalls: 'But then the two of them started fiddling around with all this new technology and electronic maps [GPS]. Next thing they're showing *me* where it is and a short cut to get there! So we agreed to follow their short cut up to a point and then I would make the call whether to carry on or turn back and follow the original road on my hand-drawn map … You know, I can still draw it with my eyes closed.'

But the short cut was spot-on. 'How I don't know,' Dippenaar says, 'but the landscape started looking familiar even though the trees were much bigger than I remembered them. All I know is that at one stage I told them, this is it, we're in the old target area. So we searched up and down but all we found were maize fields and small settlements with women and kids.'

Stefan conversed with the women in a mixture of Portuguese and the local language but they knew nothing of the battle fought so long ago. Their menfolk were across the border in Namibia to earn much-needed cash. After calling at about five villages, they were none the wiser and starting to get that sinking feeling.

'Then we finally met an old man who told us to follow him.'

Their guide showed them what the bush had kept hidden for so long – the rusted undercarriage of one of the 23 mm guns used with such devastating effect against the Ratels. They started searching the surrounding bush and soon found the old trenches almost filled in with earth and leaves over time.

'Then I knew this was the real McCoy,' recalls Dippenaar.

Those who know Dippenaar (to many veterans he is now 'Oom Dippies' rather than 'General') will tell you he always seems calm and composed. In control. For such is his nature and his style of leadership: 'But when I got into that old trench and realised this is it, and I looked up and saw the beams they used for overhead protection … that whole attack and battle fell open before me like a book. And, ja, those were very emotional moments, just thinking of so many men who died there.'

The tears flowed and Martin and Stefan respectfully gave Dippenaar some space to let his emotions go.

'You know, this was what I had set out to do. To find the objective so I could take the men back to where they had fought so hard. Because you can write all the books you want, but nothing gets close to standing on the actual ground where you know your men died. Where you once again realise, with great gratitude, how fortunate you were that the bullets missed you.

'You were there, you heard those shots, men fell around you. And you feel the fear once again. You can't explain that fear and worry to somebody else. But here you stand again and you relive it all and realise what happened here was something bigger than all of us.'

Then he went back to Pretoria and soon the WhatsApp groups were buzzing with the news: Oom Dippies found it, we're going back! Eighty or more veterans were keen to join the pilgrimage. Frantic planning followed, because it was already March and the goal was to stand on the actual ground on 10 June 2020 – the 40th anniversary of the battle for Smokeshell.

At first, Paul and HP were hesitant about going back and kicked the idea around like a football over the phone. 'I'm not going without you,' said one. 'I'll go if you go,' said the other.

Finally they both signed up for it.

'I really wanted to stand on that ground again. I knew it would mean a lot to me and HP and a lot of other guys as well. To be able to say, here we are, in this patch of bush guys fell all around me but I made it … and to honour those who died,' Paul explains.

And once again Lynette encouraged him to go.

'It's absolutely the best thing for Paul and all these men who still go through life with so much hurt inside them. The only place they can go and unload that hurt is in the bush. Nowhere else. No TV programme, no book, can give them that same sense of closure they get when they stand on that ground again. I think they all need that. I wish one could sue the defence force to sponsor those who cannot afford to go back there and call it counselling.'

HP's motivation hits you like a punch in the gut.

'Many people asked me why I want to go back there. Do I want inner peace, closure? And I tell them no. I just want to go and stand on the last place where I was fit and healthy, where my body was still whole. Before everything changed in the blink of an eye.

'I made my peace with everything a long time ago, I don't want to go and sort out some big psychological issue. But maybe going there will also help to heal my body faster, for the mind and the body work together.'

But there was one vital issue – his wound had to be painstakingly cleaned and sanitised twice a day and his colostomy bag changed. How to do that during the long haul through Namibia and in the unforgiving Angolan bush? The risk of infection was real.

Phia did not hesitate for a moment. After so many years of being wife and nurse, she was not going to let him go off to Angola without her. She has always cared for HP and she would do so in the bush as well.

'I looked forward to being there with him and to supporting him. I confess the thought of seeing him standing there was a bit daunting: I knew he would cry a lot. But all we've gone through together, all the pain and suffering, made me believe that his burden would be lighter when he returned. And, ja, just travelling with everybody would be enjoyable.'

The logistics for this physical journey into the past was not unlike that of a military operation. Off-road vehicles that could withstand the punishment of those Angolan dirt tracks, radios for communication, flights to and from Windhoek, guest houses during the long drive through Namibia, camping stuff for Angola, food, water, visas, yellow fever shots … where to refuel in Angola? The list seemed endless.

All over South Africa the community of veterans started getting things done, just like four decades ago, using whatever resources and contacts they had and innovating as needed. Ticking off things on that list one by one.

But then a new enemy cast its deadly shadow across the world. Provincial and international borders were shut down, air travel suspended and entire nations forced into lockdown. The journey back to Smokeshell was stopped dead by the Covid-19 pandemic.

14

OLD FRIENDS REUNITED AND HEALING IN THE BUSH

The planned journey back to Smokeshell was delayed for two years and three months. When the hard lockdown was eased, you could leave your home but not cross provincial boundaries. Eventually, you could leave your province but other countries were still a no-go. And finally, there would be the administrative nightmare of crossing the borders of three countries with different sets of Covid regulations, protocols and testing regimes.

As the pandemic ebbed and spiked, hopes were raised only to be dashed once again. Flights and accommodation were booked and cancelled. During this trying time, nobody was more frustrated than Dippenaar.

'Man, it was terrible. You know, various role players put a lot of effort into the tour early in 2020. Including people based in Namibia like Thys Rall.'

But just when they were about ready to go, Covid slammed the door in their faces.

And the attrition caused by the virus would prove far more harrowing than just the problem of shuttered borders. Some veterans fell ill (at least one died) and others lost income because

Covid regulations strangled the economy, killed jobs and put small businesses to the sword. Apart from Covid's death toll and the bleeding economy, there was the psychological impact.

'What really made me sad was that in 2020 I had a list of more than 80 people who committed to the Smokeshell tour. But after Covid only half of those could go. Some could not afford to anymore, others were still afraid of the disease, a whole bunch of reasons.'

HP and Phia were among those who fell ill with Covid. Ironically, the virus got its claws into them on 10 June, the anniversary of the attack on Smokeshell. Phia explains that HP was in hospital at the time, recovering from the umpteenth surgical procedure due to his wound. But after the operation, the hole in his lower back was bigger than ever.

He was lying in the same hospital where Phia worked: 'There was another patient who was discharged but felt ill only hours later. So she returned to the hospital and tested positive for Covid.'

Within a week, first Phia and then HP tested positive: 'That moment when they test you and then tell you it is positive ... that is truly terrifying. You've already heard about so many people who got the virus, so many who died from it.'

And, as a nurse, Phia was only too aware of the threat the virus posed to someone with a weakened immune system. Like her Hennie.

Today she believes it was a blessing in disguise that they contracted the virus at the same time. It meant they could isolate together and she could care for him as she always did – even though she was also ill: 'I did not feel all that bad, it was more like a very rotten cold. But old Hennie was still weak from his operation and was really ill. But we pulled through. You know, one tends to joke about how many bags of salt you've eaten together. But I can honestly say we've eaten more than you could load on even the biggest truck.'

True to her nature, this remarkable woman saw an upside to their brush with the great global killer: 'At the hospital the other staff and I were always scared of the disease. Once I had the disease, I believed, I also had a degree of immunity. So it was a turning point in our lives.'

It was February 2022 before the pandemic loosened its stranglehold sufficiently for Dippenaar to send out the word: this year we're going!

But Paul was conflicted, for a lot of water had passed under the bridge since the 2020 tour was derailed. Lynette, who was always there for him, had been diagnosed with breast cancer and undergone a double mastectomy. 'I really doubted whether it would be the right thing to go,' he says. 'I was in two minds.

'So I spoke to both Andrew Whitaker and HP and I felt encouraged to go. And then I talked to Lynette and she said, "Go, it will do you good."

'Then my passport disappeared a week before I was due to depart. And I wondered, was this a sign that I'm not supposed to go, that my wife really did not want me to go?'

He was in turmoil until Lynette discovered that her brother, who often visited their George home, had accidentally taken Paul's passport from where it was lying next to his green ID book. 'So I got my passport back, but I'm still thinking, should I go or not? Is it going to be a good thing or not?'

In the end he packed his bags.

Far away in Bloemfontein, Phia packed what she would need to

Andrew Whitaker (left) on the old battlefield, with the memorial for Smokeshell's dead brought from South Africa.

care for HP's wounds with little or no fuss. She could have done it with her eyes closed and everything was always to hand. She was far more worried about what clothes she should take as luggage would be restricted: 'I've heard that it gets terribly cold in the bush at night. I really did not want to be cold!'

In the meantime, the tour was morphing. Back in 2020, Dippenaar's plan was for a specialised Smokeshell tour: cross the border into Angola, spend a night or two at the site and hold a simple memorial service, then head home.

Now, two years later, other big guns of 61 MVA weighed in. Before you could say 'Contact!' it became part and parcel of a long tour covering the timeline of the Border War. Starting at Smokeshell in the west, the tour would proceed on a route that would cover other significant battlefields to the east, including the wreck of Mielie Meiring's Ratel near Calueque and Cuito Cuanavale.

All this was well and good because Smokeshell was a 'go' – and that's what really mattered to the men who lost their youth there.

But first we should pause to meet two more travellers.

BIG-HEARTED ANDREW WHITAKER

More than 40 years ago, this Eastern Cape 'soutie' would have been lean and fit. Nowadays, his long, snowy hair and beard give him the appearance of a kindly Santa Claus.

But when it comes to South African men of a certain age, looks can be deceiving. Andrew was not at the very tip of the spear like Paul Louw's platoon on 10 June 1980, but he was in the second wave: Alpha Company, Platoon 2.

'It was late afternoon and we had just made contact with the enemy when our Ratel got hung up on a big tree stump right in the middle of the target area. We were stranded. There was AK-47 fire coming at us all the time but a decision was made not to return fire as it would give away our position. We camouflaged our Ratel as best we could and tried to scrape out trenches in the hard earth without making noise.'

The rest of that day and the entire night they hunkered down as sporadic fighting raged all around them: 'At about eight o'clock that night a section from Bravo Company joined us, and for the first time we heard the horrific story of how they suffered 13 dead and many more wounded.

'About two in the morning we heard the enemy withdraw from their nearby position with a sound like heavy chains dragging over the ground. We assumed they were towing away one of those 23 mil cannons.'

At sunrise on day two they did a sweeping foot patrol and discovered that the feared Swapo gun was deployed only 200 m from where their Ratel was still stranded: 'Much later that day our Ratel was freed and we could rejoin our company. Only then did we hear the names of the dead. Even though we were not in the same company, I knew them all. During basic training I was in the same bungalow as Paul Kruger, Steve Cronjé and Frank Lello. During second phase I was with Andrew Madden, Mike Luyt, Pip Warrener and Rob de Vito. Lieutenant Hannes du Toit was also with us for a while.'

In the melting pot of the mechanised infantry, just about everybody crossed paths at one stage or another. Junior officers, gunners, drivers, you name it. And now, so many years after Smokeshell, the former rifleman from the Eastern Cape took Paul, HP and Phia under his wing. Andrew, the owner of a family chartered accountancy firm, assumed responsibility for their transport and accommodation on the long haul from Windhoek to Smokeshell and back, with special care for HP's comfort.

In times of peace, roles are often reversed, for Father Time does not care whether you were a lieutenant, commandant or common troopie.

NICOLA DICKSON, PASTORAL THERAPIST AND RESEARCHER

Nicky was only 22 months old when her parents relocated from Britain to Comptonville, in the southwestern parts of Johannesburg. While growing up, Nicky, just like every member of her generation, knew somebody who was doing his army stint: uncles, cousins, brothers, boyfriends, school friends. 'Society was quite militarised at the time,' she recalls.

As children, she and her friends played in the koppies of Naturena, a residential area not far from Soweto: 'We often saw lorries filled with troops. We never knew where they were going, but in our young minds there was something heroic about them. At Mondeor High we had school cadets and shooting on Fridays. I was a cadet leader and even considered going to the Army Women's College in George ... Such was life in South Africa back then.'

Like many South African teenage girls, she wrote letters to troopies 'somewhere on the Border' and doused the envelopes with Charlie perfume. But it was only when her future husband, Graham, was called up for a Citizen Force camp in the operational area that she realised how the war affected relationships, careers and families – and how important those letters were.

As time passed, she got her master's degree in psychology while raising two kids. Then, one day in 2004, her parents-in-law dropped off Graham's old army trunk, stuffed with uniforms and other bits and pieces of equipment. Their son Luke was fascinated by the contents and decided to join the British army, as his dad hailed from Scotland.

Meanwhile, Graham had a friend who still struggled with nightmares after his experiences in the Border War. And in 2009 the two men travelled back to the places where they had served in browns. Nicky recalls: 'They studied maps and planned their route. And when they returned, Graham's friend had no more nightmares.'

By that time she was a practising pastoral therapist, and the trip got her thinking about the value of returning to the place where you experienced trauma. The following year, 2010, Graham joined a 61 Mech veterans' tour to Angola. His tales of emotional nights unburdening around campfires under the Angolan stars, and of memorial crosses fixed to baobab trees, further inspired her. 'I've always been fascinated by rituals and symbolism,' she explains.

Nicky decided to do her doctoral research on the trauma and healing of Border War veterans. She wanted to explore the 'cowboys don't cry' mentality among the men, and the SADF's apparent failure to provide adequate counselling to those who were pushed into the firing line back then.

'It was always my plan to return with some of these men to the places where it all happened, because I started to realise how meaningful that was.' And when she heard of Dippenaar's obsession with taking the men he had once led back to Smokeshell, she knew this was her chance to be an eyewitness in the bush, not only as a researcher but as the wife of a veteran and the mother of a young soldier going through a tough time in the UK.

Nicky was as frustrated as the veterans when Covid became a massive roadblock on their road to healing. She was grateful when the restrictions on gatherings and travel were relaxed to the point where she could attend a Smokeshell reunion in Bloemfontein.

Then, finally, it was time to head off to the bush.

OLD FRIENDS REUNITED IN TSUMEB

To get things back on track after all the bureaucratic frustrations of the pandemic was not easy – especially as Smokeshell was now part of a much bigger tour.

So it was not until early July 2022 – and no longer June, when the battle took place – that the small Smokeshell delegation gathered in Windhoek. Andrew Whitaker, who had driven up from the Eastern Cape, collected Paul, HP and Phia at the airport. They were to be his passengers for the journey to Smokeshell and back to Windhoek.

In Windhoek, the tour group first attended a dinner in their honour laid on by the Namibian MOTHs, led by André

Anthonissen, a great friend to all 61 Mech veterans. In his welcoming speech, André quoted the words Paul had uttered in an interview with the journalist Willemien Brümmer: 'Jy mag maar voor jou Ratel huil.' (It's okay to cry in front of your Ratel.) As a humorous touch, tour members were presented with small packets of tissues, accompanied by sage advice: 'Keep it handy because you *are* going to cry!'

From Windhoek, they headed north in a convoy of bakkies and other sturdy private vehicles. Next stop was Tsumeb, the town whose destiny had been so closely intertwined with that of 61 Mech during the war. And there, a joyous reunion took place between HP and Reinhard Friederich, a farmer of the district.

As described in my book *Tannie Pompie se Oorlog*, the Triangle of Death (the area between the towns of Tsumeb, Grootfontein and Otavi) was infiltrated by a large group of Swapo guerrillas in 1982. One of the insurgent groups set a well-planned ambush just off the cutline at Tsintsabis, about 70 km northeast of Tsumeb.

They destroyed a Ratel with a hail of rocket-propelled grenades, killing five 61 Mech troops and three members of the Tsumeb farm commando. The Tsumeb men who died in that inferno were Daantjie van der Westhuizen from the farm Koedoesvlei, his son-in-law Hendrik Potgieter and their legendary farm-worker-turned-tracker, Jan Kausab.

It was the opening salvo of the counterinsurgency operation named Yahoo. The tight-knit Tsumeb farm community would bury six loved ones before it was all over; 61 Mech's losses would total nine national servicemen. Swapo's losses would amount to 71 killed.

Reinhard, one of the Tsumeb commando's best trackers, was luckier. He detonated a landmine while running on the spoor of

A happy reunion in Tsumeb between Reinhard Friederich, the local farmer who detonated a landmine in 1982, and HP Ferreira, who did so much to lift his spirits in Pretoria's 1 Military Hospital.

insurgents and lived to tell the tale. Like many casualties of the Border War, he was airlifted to Grootfontein and on to 1 Military Hospital in Pretoria.

Reinhard grew up on a farm and spent his boyhood with San hunters, learning their language and wilderness arts. As an adult he continued to immerse himself in San culture. And now he found himself lying in a hospital ward, pining for the sights, sounds and smells of the bush he loved so much. He was deeply depressed.

But one fellow patient would have none of this. HP, in hospital for a year already, recognised Reinhard as one of the farmers who had shown him and his buddies warm hospitality when they patrolled his land in the happier days before Smokeshell. He regularly wheeled his way to Reinhard's bed and regaled him with jokes and stories.

Reinhard will tell you today that HP was his saving grace during those long, depressing months while the shrapnel wounds in his legs healed, and how upbeat and caring HP was towards others, in spite of his own terrible injuries. And now, more than 40 years later, here they were embracing in Tsumeb.

'Jislaaik, I was so emotional when I saw him. He looks just like when I last saw him. Such a big, strong man,' HP says. Dippenaar, too, was elated to see the stubborn farmer who once stomped into his HQ and tried to tell him how to run a counterinsurgency war.

In a shady guest house garden, the three men and Reinhard's wife, Yvonne, chewed the cud and relived the past. They got teary-eyed but they also laughed a lot. 'To see them together like that, the joy of their reunion, was one of my personal highlights of the tour,' says Andrew, who had let Reinhard know that HP would be in town.

One more thing remained to be done before the tour group left Tsumeb, with all its bittersweet memories.

Riana van der Westhuizen was only 11 years old when her dad and brother-in-law died in that burning Ratel near the cutline at Tsintsabis. And shortly before the tour group pulled into Tsumeb, the exact ambush spot – no more than a small clearing in the bush – had been rediscovered. Now Riana travelled from her home in Swakopmund to stand on that spot for the first time.

During a small ceremony she, her nephew Danie and a few of the 61 Mech veterans fixed a cross to a tree trunk in memory of her father and brother-in-law, and also of her mother, the legendary Tannie Pompie van der Westhuizen, who worked as a military signaller from her farm kitchen during the war. When Pompie died years later, some people say, it was from a broken heart.

The tour group's campsite at the old Smokeshell battlefield in Angola.

That moment in the small clearing near the forgotten cutline was a marker on Riana's long road to healing. And for the handful of 61 Mech veterans present, it was an opportunity to honour the family who welcomed so many national servicemen with open arms on their farm Koedoesvlei. A family remembered as heroes for the enormous sacrifices they made.

Then it was time to move on.

Border crossings of the legal kind can be a drag at the best of times, but this was something else. First there was the bureaucratic maze of Covid certificates on the Angolan side. Then the customs officers got an eyeful of the memorial the South Africans had brought along to erect on the hallowed earth of Smokeshell.

It may have been the four legs of the specially designed and constructed object that alarmed them: replicas of R1 and AK-47 assault rifles cut from sheet metal, one at each corner of the base. But they were clearly not real weapons. More likely it was the 90 mm cannon round on top (a harmless dud) that took some explaining. The plaques in English and Portuguese identifying this as a memorial to the dead on both sides of the conflict seemed to make little impression at first.

Whatever the case was, it took Jaap Steyn – another former commander of 61 Mech – a short lifetime to sort it out.

Finally, all 39 tour members and the memorial made it through customs and into Angola. That night, the group camped about 50 km on the far side of the town of Ongiva. Up to now, Andrew had arranged comfortable lodgings for his three passengers as they travelled up through Namibia. Here in Angola, a queen-sized inflatable mattress in the back of Andrew's SUV would serve as HP's 'hotel suite'. For Phia there was a small tent, while Andrew and Paul made do with stretchers and sleeping bags under the stars.

Then the sun rose and it was 9 July. Time for the last push to the old killing field.

At times, Paul will testify, it was as if the Angolan roads were wreaking revenge on the old invaders from the southern tip of Africa. They swayed and bumped and got reacquainted with every rattling bone in their bodies.

'Jissie, that stretch of road was pounded into nothing. And I'm talking about the main road! And the dust … When one vehicle pulled away the next one had to wait ten minutes for the dust to settle before it could follow.

'Then we got to the turnoff Stefan van Wyk marked for us earlier. And that was when the going really got tough. We had to follow a dirt track weaving around the villages, just like the one we bundu-bashed with the Ratels way back then. And that stretch of track gave us hell for another three, four hours until we got where we were going.'

The local chief was there, having waited god knows how long

for them to arrive. Andrew gingerly pulled off the track and edged his SUV into a small clearing in the bush marked by Stefan before he departed on some personal errand.

They got out, stretched their tortured limbs then slowly looked around, trying to drink it all in. This is it. Finally. Somewhere behind the screen of bush is where it all happened.

But Paul felt no connection to the place.

'As soon as we stopped, HP wanted to go to a spot where Oom Dippies said he found a rusty old R1 magazine, some exploded 20 mil rounds and pieces of armoured glass … a place where South African forces must have been. So we walked there but nothing about the landscape was familiar.'

The sun was setting when they got to a spot where they, too, found some old cartridge cases and pieces of glass. Dippenaar believed this was where Paul and HP's Ratel burned to a blackened hulk, but Paul was not convinced. He had a sneaking suspicion Dippenaar did not want them to stand on the actual spot until the next morning – 10 July, exactly 42 years and one month since the battle.

'But okay, we did find some stuff there … Oom Dippies later explained he believed this was where they towed my Ratel after it was recovered – not the actual spot where it was hit.'

The way Nicky saw it, with her trained psychologist's eye, Paul was not offhand and sceptical at all.

'The vehicle I travelled in broke down on that bad road and had to be towed in. So it was late afternoon by the time we arrived at the camp site. The first thing I saw was the guys heading off into the bush. They were going to the spot where it was said Paul's Ratel burned, I heard. I asked if I could join them.

'Paul was in the lead, looked hurried and intense as he followed this little path. Andrew followed and HP, with his walking stick, lagged behind. I had the feeling Paul was anxious to get there. Suddenly we were in a small clearing among the trees where the earth seemed scorched, ringed only by sparse tufts of grass.

'Paul and HP scratched around in the dirt, picking up pieces of glass and metal, which they turned over in their hands and discussed at length. Then HP started drawing the outline of a Ratel in the dirt with his walking stick while explaining, this is the direction we were going when we were hit; here was my driver's seat; there the side door where the others leaped and some got cut down.

'It does not take much for HP to show his emotions but this time it was Paul who truly let go, as if he was finally free. He fell to his knees and put his arms around HP and asked his forgiveness. Both sobbed intensely. After that they walked off in different directions, as if they needed space to regain their composure. HP said he needed to pray in solitude.'

For HP, the bush did not bear any resemblance to the place where he was so young and fit before the enemy fire tore through him and he lost all awareness of what was happening around him.

'The trees were much bigger than those in the old pictures I've seen. So in that way it's not the same bush. But when you walk past one of those old trenches, that's when it hits you. You feel it, you start getting those flashbacks. You know, like the terror in the eyes of that guy looking back at me just before I drove over him ... it's not a good feeling.'

Even as his own emotions surged, his concern was for his former lieutenant. 'I felt so sorry for old Paul, he was so heartbroken.'

For long moments a heavy silence pressed down on the little group in the clearing. Then Paul said he wanted to walk and asked Nicky to accompany him.

There was also time for sightseeing. At Lake Otjikoto in Namibia are (from left) Johann Dippenaar, Paul Louw, HP and Phia Ferreira and Andrew Whitaker.

61 Mech veterans during the memorial service on the old Smokeshell battlefield in Angola.

Old cartridge cases and a fragment of armoured glass found by HP and Paul where their Ratel burned.

The Smokeshell memorial, with the carriage of the old 23 mm gun partly visible on the left.

HP (right) and Gerhard van Rooyen play traditional boeremusiek during an overnight stop in Angola.

'We talked about his feelings and how his heart raced as he approached the clearing where it was said his Ratel burned. And about his guilt because he felt he made the wrong decisions. It's a normal reaction to trauma. What if I did this instead of that? Would things have turned out differently? I think it was a good emotional unburdening.'

They trudged back to the vehicle, pitched camp and had supper. Nicky and Paul stayed up till midnight: 'We talked about his dad, his role model, who also served in the army. We talked about all the father figures in his life. How he and HP switched roles, for it was HP who took the lead to bring Paul and the other veterans together again.'

Then they all said their good nights and went off to their separate beds, such as they were. Tomorrow was going to be a big day and they all needed some doss.

But Paul's demons were waiting in ambush. And they pounced as he lay on his borrowed stretcher under the same stars where he spent a terrifying night so long ago.

He fought through it all again. His order to drive out of the riverbed. The shock when he realised they were among the enemy's gun positions. The explosions and fire and smoke inside the Ratel and the smell of fresh blood. And always that burning question: what if?

Then he was jerked back to the present by a gunshot somewhere in the middle distance, and his anxiety was all about the here and now. The chief who met them on arrival seemed friendly, but what if others resented their return to this place? How was he going keep his travelling companions safe if they were attacked?

His relief when the sun reared its head and the demons retreated was boundless – just like 42 years earlier, at the end of a long night huddled inside the immobilised Ratel surrounded by the enemy camp fires.

Paul could have kissed that big soutie Andrew when he walked around the nose of the bakkie and remarked wryly: 'I can see the demons were busy with you last night.'

Only metres away, HP had a restful night thanks to the sleeping pill he habitually took. But when he crawled from his 'suite' in the back of Andrew's SUV he needed no telling that Paul had had a rough time of it.

'That stretcher of his was ripped lengthways. I have no idea how he managed that, maybe he was tossing and turning a lot, but it was ripped from head to toe. We just abandoned it right there.'

Straight off, Paul wanted to know if anybody else heard the gunshot in the night. Nobody did. In the reassuring light of day, he realised it was probably just a hunter or somebody driving predators away from his livestock. But in the dark of night he instinctively reverted to the young lieutenant who wanted to protect his troops.

Early-morning coffee was brewed and drunk in contemplative silence. Then it was time to take their folding chairs and follow the path to the big tree where the memorial had already been placed, covered by a 61 Mech veterans' banner, ready for the unveiling. For the date was 10 July.

Other tour members converged at the tree and set down their chairs in a crescent shape. Now Nicky, the observer and researcher, assumed a pastoral role, for Jaap Steyn had asked her to do the scripture reading. But first she constructed an altar of sorts at the foot of the memorial.

'Because of my love of symbols and rituals, I packed candles for people to light before I left home. I also picked up pieces of metal and twigs at the spot where HP drew the Ratel outline in the dirt the previous afternoon.'

What struck her during the service was the bateleur eagle circling overhead: 'The two other women in the group saw it as well. For me it was a sign that, okay, God is here.'

Each member of the group of 39 got the chance to contribute to the service in their own way. 'Emotional' is the word HP uses over and over when describing that morning on the hallowed ground of Smokeshell: 'It was like closing a book.'

When it was his turn to talk, the words simply poured out from somewhere: 'What was uppermost in my mind was that I never wanted to see a monument to the ugly things of life again. So many killed, ours and theirs … There's nothing good about that and I never, ever want to see it again. May God spare me from that. Let us rather erect monuments to celebrate the good and beautiful things.'

It is not in HP's nature to pray in public, 'but that day I did and again the words just came naturally. And that's when I realised that I had to try and make a difference. I had to go reach out to guys who were still held captive by these things and say to them, come, let us talk about it.' Because he knew all too well there were blood brothers out there who needed help to slay the demons that still haunted them after 42 years.

Afterwards, he went to Paul and said: 'Now I've finally buried our brothers.' It was a closure he could never have hoped to find in Bloemfontein. It had to happen here, on this ground.

And Paul, despite the purgatory of the previous night, also felt a new inner peace take hold.

'When we got to where they placed the monument under the

tree, I realised this is it, now we're on the real spot. We were among the old trenches and gun emplacements and the undercarriage of that old 23 mil gun was still there. All the right signs ...

'We gathered there on the old battlefield and looked each other in the eye and said, now we are content. We stood on this ground and bade our fallen comrades farewell. I felt lighter when we finally drove away. It had to happen.'

A big relief for Paul was to see how HP, over whose wounds he felt so much guilt, was emotionally strengthened by the experience: 'He was a different person, it radiated from him. And I think Phia, after caring for him all these years, also understood for the first time how it happened to him ... the difficult terrain and circumstances we were up against.'

What about the career officer who left no stone unturned to get his former national servicemen back to the place where their lives changed so brutally?

In his response, Johann Dippenaar is as calm and composed as ever, but he admits: 'It was emotional. Seeing somebody like HP there on the spot where he almost died and after so many medical procedures, and his wife Phia there to support him. That's not something you see every day. It was unique and exceptional.'

It was an unforgettable experience to see and hear each man there tell his story: 'You just knew how deeply it touched each one of them, you could see it. And it had a deeply profound impact on me.'

Witnessing it all, he could not help but dwell on that moment in March 2020 when he realised he had finally found the lost battlefield: 'To stand there, more than two years after we found that rusty old piece of the Swapo gun, and now the memorial we brought with us is standing right next to it ... unbelievable.'

Dippenaar also feels a deep sense of gratitude to the villagers who, first, guided them to the old gun emplacements and, second, allowed them to camp and erect the memorial on their land.

But as soon as the rituals of mourning and healing under the tree were over, Dippenaar departed with haste. For there was bad news from the home front: his wife, Hannelie, was seriously ill.

Shortly afterwards, the rest of the tour group also split up. Nicky joined the larger group, led by Jaap Steyn, for the rest of the extended Angolan battlefield tour: Protea, Cassinga, Askari, Cuito Cuanavale, Calueque ...

Andrew, however, had arranged something special for Paul, HP and Phia. In the relative comfort of his Mercedes 4x4, they headed straight back to Namibia.

15
REFLECTIONS

Maps of the operational area of the former South West Africa show that Dippenaar built his base above the northeastern corner of the world-famous Etosha Game Reserve.

War can be cruel to wild animals, but sometimes soldiers draw spiritual comfort from nature and its creatures. While Omuthiya was taking shape under the camelthorn trees, the young troopies sometimes gazed in wonder at elephants moving soundlessly through the base at night. And Reinhard Friederich will tell you that the nearby reserve is a magical place. Before detonating that landmine during Operation Yahoo, he wandered Etosha on foot, recording the stories and secrets of the last San who lived there in their own language of musical clicks.

It was to this paradise that the survivors of Paul's platoon were sent to do routine patrols after the hellish battle for Smokeshell. For some, such as Jan Verhoef, those peaceful days of counting game with conservation officials and hearty meals from farm kitchens were balm for their damaged souls.

And Etosha is where Andrew now took Paul, HP and Phia after going through the emotional wringer amid the old trenches and bunkers at the place they will forever know as Smokeshell.

The big man from the Eastern Cape did some research during the planning stages of the tour and discovered that the reserve offered reasonable bed-and-breakfast rates for South Africans. So he booked his charges and himself in for four nights.

There, during game drives along the glistening white salt pans, at the waterhole viewing sites and around crackling camp fires, they dissected what they had just experienced in the Angolan bush. What they felt and what it meant. Hard questions and honest answers, no holding back. Paul, who was no stranger to questions that stung, found it therapeutic.

'Man, I tell you, it was a real unburdening. I think if we'd headed straight for Windhoek airport from Angola the whole tour would have turned out less meaningful than it did. We talked about all the stuff we kept bottled up inside for so long, but in a relaxed way. No tension, no issues.

'I have to admit old Andrew knew what he was doing. He knew something like this would be necessary, but it never even crossed my mind before we got there.'

The kindly Andrew also knew it would be HP and Phia's first proper holiday in ten years owing to his medical challenges. Now, more than ever, a break was called for. HP needed a respite from all the hard driving that caused him considerable back pain and discomfort. And Phia, the 24/7 nurse and wife, needed a break, period. 'It was lovely, I really enjoyed it,' she said about her first game reserve stay. She shared cellphone videos of pangolins, rhinos, elephants and lions.

But let's catch up with the pastoral therapist and researcher before we learn what the four companions gleaned from all that soul-searching in Etosha.

Nicky Dickson and Johann Dippenaar at Club Omuthiya in Bloemfontein after their return from Angola.

NICKY

She was loath to say goodbye to Andrew, Paul, HP, Phia and Dippenaar there at the Smokeshell campsite: 'It was all too sudden. Everybody I built a relationship with was just gone, I so wanted to talk to them about it all.'

All was not lost, however. She missed out on Etosha's fireside debriefings but more rituals and symbolism awaited on the rest of the extended Angolan tour she now embarked on.

When her husband, Graham, went on the 2010 veterans' tour, he took with him a number of wooden crosses made by her father-in-law. These were fixed to trees at significant sites along the route after being signed by the members of the tour, including Graham. 'I was so happy to discover that some of these crosses in the bush were still there after so many years,' Nicky says.

Now, in 2022, they also erected a small memorial at the

place where Louis Harmse – Paul Louw's company commander at Smokeshell – died on 24 August 1981, during Operation Protea. Harmse was about to toss a grenade into an enemy bunker at Xangongo when he was shot and killed at close range by a concealed Swapo fighter. He was 27. (His father, Colonel Desmond Harmse, died in a plane crash in Angola during Operation Savannah in 1975.)

Nicky's last night in Angola was spent camping under two huge baobab trees known to the 61 Mech community as Blackie's Place. There, she felt a strong connection to her husband, for it was Graham's tale of the emotional cleansing on that very spot in 2010 that had inspired her doctoral research on the healing of Border War veterans.

After the tour, at the next Smokeshell reunion in Bloemfontein, she sat down for a debriefing with HP and Andrew. With Paul in George she did a video interview from her Johannesburg home: 'There was a sense that the journey was what they needed to get closure and make sense of it all. The emotional pain never goes away, but it's about learning how to live with it.'

At the time this book was being written, she was awaiting the final word from the academic committee reviewing her doctoral thesis.

'I think my research is a microcosm of the trauma of all Border War veterans. For so long there was this man-thing not to talk about it. But in the meantime our society underwent dramatic change … and now you have this outpouring of traumatic stories, but what do you do with it? Where do you create a space for it in a society which marginalises veterans? Many ordinary soldiers became collateral damage of the political changes of 1994, while professional officers just carried on with their careers.'

She believes veterans' gatherings are essential because no other public space exists for them to share what they went through. Spaces where they can just be who they are and be heard.

And, yes, when she finally saw them on the soil where everything happened to them so long ago, the therapeutic value was evident: 'They had to go back to the place where everything changed for them in order to confront it.'

Nicky, too, will never be the same after hearing their stories. 'The privilege of going back there with them has changed me.'

ANDREW

The big guy started attending the Bloemfontein *skouerskure* around 2014 and grew close to HP: 'I knew how important it was for HP, and also Paul, to return to Smokeshell – much more important than it was for me. And after everything that HP sacrificed, I would do anything to help him get there.

'His faith is so strong and his biggest goal in life is to help others. So he absolutely deserved the opportunity to go back there, and Phia with him. It was very special to see them there. Paul had a very rough night, but I think he got a bit more closure. Even Dippies was emotional.'

For Andrew, the four days in Etosha were the perfect end to the Smokeshell tour. 'Sometimes we don't realise how privileged we are, we take so much for granted. It really hit me when I heard it was HP and Phia's first-ever visit to a game reserve. We relaxed, enjoyed wonderful game viewing and just talked.'

And he confesses that when he left the Smokeshell site, after the memorial service under the tree, he thought that was it, done and dusted. He's not going back there again. But since then he's had a change of heart: 'I'd like to take my wife there so she can experience what Phia and Nicky did. She met them after the tour and listened to their stories. You know, at first I thought the tour was not really for women, but now I think differently.'

He would also like to explore the old battlefield a bit more. Who knows, maybe he'll find the exact spot where he and his buddies spent a night next to their stranded Ratel while the bullets came from all sides.

PAUL

'You know, for 42 years I blamed myself. That feeling of guilt never went away. People tell me it was not my fault, and it probably was not. Nobody else can really say with certainty that my decision in that moment was wrong.

'You tend to think these things only happen in movies ... But as a Christian I believe what was meant to happen, happened. That there were lessons I and definitely others had to learn. For 28 years I cut it out of my thinking, but when I finally started talking about it, I started seeing things in perspective.

'I now see a higher hand in three things that happened that day. One, the fact that I was not severely wounded meant I could take control and look out for the others. Two, the fact that HP was medically evacuated so soon after he was shot. And lastly, my Bravo section [Section 2, of Ratel 21B] clearing all those enemy trenches without picking up even the slightest scratch ... I still can't believe it. So, yes, there was definitely a higher hand involved.'

The return to Smokeshell was his only – and very tailored – experience of a 61 Mech veterans' tour: 'But to put it in a nutshell, it's a good thing. Whether it's about closure or verifying history for yourself.'

And, ja, it has therapeutic value above and beyond the kind you will experience on a shrink's couch: 'You have to go and stand on the place where the trauma happened, there's just no avoiding that. You have to stand there and say, this is where it happened. But ja, it took us a long time to get there.'

Paul would return to Smokeshell again 'but only if they fly me in by chopper', he jokes. 'The journey was exhausting. It's a torturous road and at our age the pounding you take in a vehicle is not fun at all.

'But therapeutically its one hundred per cent worth it to visit the place and talk to people who lived through the same thing as you did.'

HP

He often claims he's far better at using his hands than his mind. Be that as it may, around the campfires of Etosha he came into his own as a philosopher.

'I believe when you have a healthy mind, your body will have an easier time of it. But if the psyche is battling, so will the flesh. Nou ja, after standing at Smokeshell the psyche is doing well … the only thing that can hurt it is the pain your body feels. The pain takes away from the psyche if you allow it to; it can be like a shout in your mind.'

HP is thankful that Phia, who supported him unconditionally for so long, now has a better understanding of what happened back then: 'This adventure you went on was actually hell. You went to kill people and the reward was in winning. But you had no idea it would damage and haunt you later in life. You see so many people who still hurt inside because of the war, because they can't forget or make their peace with it.'

HP and Phia at the spot where he was shot in his
Ratel in 1980.

Phia looks on as HP and Paul Louw pick up debris from their
destroyed Ratel.

He sleeps better at night since returning from Smokeshell. And that fateful date, 10 June, is 'just like a birthday now, it doesn't bother me like it used to'.

'What saddens me is that our whole generation was so ignorant about the things we did. You were taught not to question things. You had a job to do, you were told how to do it, and then you went and did it. And you believed in what you did. That's how we were raised. Out of respect for your elders you never talked back or asked why – and maybe that was a mistake.

'You know, I'm not saying the war should never have happened. I'm saying if we were better informed there may have been that guy who spoke out and said, no, let's rather do it differently. And if that happened, maybe we would have found an easier way to establish a proper peace.'

Today, in his mid-60s, he often reflects on 'that *domgeit* [stupidity] we had. I mean, I did not really know what I was going to do at Smokeshell, so why go do it? But you respected your officers and corporals, you thought they knew more than you did. You believed you had to go and do your job the best you could.'

At the Smokeshell campsite, he was heartbroken when he saw what a tortured night Paul endured: 'But ja, I think it did old Paul and all of us a lot of good. We cried a good many tears, Paul and I, but those tears cleanse the soul.'

The two of them are now even closer than before: 'The fact that Paul picked me up and tossed me into the passing medical Ratel when he thought I was dead … that's why I love him so much. He cared for what he believed was my dead body and my humanity. Paul and I are close, very close. When I'm battling and I phone him late at night and hear his voice, I have the strength to go on again.'

The tour left him with a strong desire to reach out to Smokeshell veterans who also needed to go back but did not: 'There are still many guys who need help. I believe I can use what I learned from the tour to help them.'

By 'them' he means guys who are alone, without the support of a Phia a Lynette or a Pamela in their lives. Men who remain withdrawn from everyone around them: 'Alone is the worst thing, because that's when you could be driven to do something irresponsible or harm yourself.'

'Maybe I was meant to be shot so that I could gain the insight and knowledge to help other veterans in trouble. To say to somebody, hey pal, it's not the end of the world. Do this and that and you'll feel better. Carry on with your life.'

He still sees the *skouerskure* he enticed guys like Paul and Andrew to join as key: 'That's where you haul out the hurt and talk about it. And the older you get, the more you realise that is exactly what you have to do. Get it out of you because you are running out of time.'

Club Omuthiya is tucked away in a corner of Tempe Military Base on the outskirts of Bloemfontein. Named after the base Dippenaar built under the camelthorn trees just north of Etosha, it is where Smokeshell veterans gather every 10th of June.

At first glance it resembles a rectangular brick schoolroom. But on one side of a small square of hard-packed dirt stands a Ratel, one of the survivors of Smokeshell, eternally vigilant on a concrete slab.

Inside, the walls are covered with the memorabilia of a war. One end is taken up by a bar; there's a long family table in the centre and a memorial corner. It has the feel of a museum, social club and informal chapel combined.

On Marco Caforio's cellphone, always at his fingertips, are the faces and names of the Smokeshell dead.

Veterans of all units and battles are welcome here, but the echoes of Smokeshell fill every corner. And on a freezing winter day, one year after the tour back to the old Angolan battlefield, Smokeshell veterans gather here once more.

General Dippenaar is here, exuding his usual air of quiet authority and dignity. So are HP, Phia and Andrew. And Nicky and Graham. Paul could not make it because of personal and work commitments.

Today, the dirt square outside the clubhouse serves as a parade ground. A chair is placed in the middle of the square for HP to sit while he awaits the rest of his brothers. And here they come, marching in threes and led by a pipe band. Some are kitted out in regulation veteran dress, others in whatever they feel like. Hairlines have receded and waistlines expanded, but pride squares their shoulders as they halt, do a right turn and dress ranks on HP.

This year there's something special on the programme. They are to receive their *messies* (daggers), a much-cherished merit badge awarded to all who served operationally with 61 Mech. Unique to the unit, it was introduced only after the Smokeshell generation klaared out. Dippenaar slowly moves down the ranks and pins the badge, with its dagger and lightning bolts, to their chests. HP rises from his chair and stands at attention when Dippenaar reaches him.

Family members of the deceased accept the merit badges posthumously on behalf of their loved ones. Then it is time to lay wreaths next to the Ratel.

Later, the braai fires are lit and cooler boxes opened. Old stories are retold, the wives chat and children play. Laughter turns to tears and that's okay because there's no judgement here – only brotherhood born from shared experiences and mutual understanding, nothing more and nothing less.

Here, HP and Phia are the proverbial older brother and sister. He mans the spitbraai and bastes the lamb while she fusses over the salads and ranks of freshly baked farm breads. Reserved but friendly, she's treated with warm respect by all. Andrew tries to get everybody to sit down for a slide show but they're too busy catching up. Later, HP picks up his guitar and plays, just like he did in the Angolan bush.

Over a glass of red wine, Nicky and I agree what a special and

At the annual memorial day at Club Omuthiya, with an original Smokeshell Ratel as backdrop. From left: Jaap Steyn (last officer commanding 61 Mech); Elna van der Walt (widow of Smokeshell veteran Cobus van der Walt); Johann Dippenaar; parabat veteran Chappies van Zyl; Hennie 'HP' Ferreira; and Siegfried Marais of the SA Defence Force Association (with child). Behind them is Smokeshell veteran and master of ceremonies Mike Bond.

important place Club Omuthiya is. A safe haven, a community hall, a place to connect and share experiences. To talk about how your life was shaped by what you went through and how your thoughts and views about it all evolved.

Where you leave politics outside the door and rub shoulders with people who understand what you are talking about, because you are members of a brotherhood forged in fire and blood.

AN UNPLANNED TRILOGY

I find it hard to believe that I'm about to complete *Blood Brothers*, my third book about the Border War.

My own stint as a transport lance corporal at 61 Mech was a spa holiday compared to what so many other veterans of this unique unit went through.

After klaaring out in 1983, I worked as a military correspondent for the *Pretoria News* until the end of the Border War in 1989. As such, you mostly wrote what the SADF propaganda machine allowed you to write under the restrictions of the Official Secrets Act.

After that, I did not really think of the army at all for about 15 years. Until one day in 2010 when one Gert Minnaar invited *Rapport* to send a journalist along on a veterans' tour back to Angola. The journalist who got the assignment was me. Only when I arrived at the assembly point did I realise that the tour was a project by members of my old national service unit.

The journey was gripping from a historical point of view and it was deeply moving to witness the emotional healing it brought to some of my travel companions. It also enabled me to learn so much more of the bigger picture of which I was once a minuscule part. And I had the opportunity to stand on the Angolan ground where I, too, once lost a comrade.

A note is called for here. One of my travelling companions was Mike Beyl, who expressed his frustration that the tour did not include the old Smokeshell battlefield. From him I gathered that the exact location was unknown. Be that as it may, from this tour flowed a series of newspaper articles and a book, *Tannie Pompie se Oorlog*.

And that's that, I thought. But no.

For in 2018 I found myself on yet another 61 Mech veterans' tour to Angola. Like the first one, it was an amazing experience – but for completely different reasons. One thing was the same, though: we travelled through a huge swathe of Angola, visiting every significant battlefield of 61 Mech's war with the notable exception of Smokeshell. This time around, the frustration of veterans like Mike Beyl, Marco Caforio, Kelvin Luke and others was even more evident.

Anyway. The 2018 tour inspired more articles and my second book, *Die Brug*. And this time I was really done with the war, as I told my long-suffering publisher, Annie Olivier.

Famous last words, as they say. For in 2020 the grapevine started buzzing with the news that Oom Dippies had gone and found the place. What place? You know, Smokeshell. And he's going to take his guys back there.

I was moved by the thought that those who fought in 61 Mech's first battle and suffered so much also had the longest wait to go back. So ja, I signed up for the tour.

Then the pandemic messed up the world. By the time Covid retreated I, like many others on the original list, could not go. But the important thing is that those who most needed to go did so.

For Mike Beyl, it was a case of third time lucky, and he could also take his wife, Yvonne.

I am immensely grateful that I could still write this third book. It was impossible to tell the stories of every Smokeshell veteran – even though they all deserve to be told. Not because they want to evoke sympathy or boast, but simply to be heard.

I had to make the difficult decision to concentrate on Paul Louw and the men of Platoon 1, who went through the worst of the meat grinder. It is my hope that their story will in one way or another represent the stories of all who took part in that battle.

Because the Smokeshell generation has not been overlooked by Father Time, life keeps happening. Johann Dippenaar hurried back from Angola to be at Hannelie's side, but sadly she lapsed into a coma from which she never awakened.

When I visited Paul and Lynette in George, she was friendly and focused on her own healing after a double mastectomy. After my interview with Gareth Rutherford, who could not go on the tour, he lost his dad, who suffered from dementia. Gareth is still based in Swellendam but spends a lot of time on the road for work.

And on 16 September 2023, Paul lost the mother who raised him alone and with such dedication. Jo Hartman (93) died from her injuries after she was engulfed by a huge wave in a Wilderness parking area.

My sincere condolences and best wishes to you all.

And Jan Hoevers? During the Covid lockdown, the self-made king of Great Brak's builders bought a European canal boat online. While his old comrades were returning to Smokeshell, he was cruising the canals of France and the Netherlands with his wife, Ricky.

When they returned, Jan, ever on the lookout for a new project, had another boat built – this time to take visitors and school kids on excursions on the Great Brak River, which meanders to the sea far below his castle.

Marco Caforio was another who could not join the tour. He and his skydiving team paid tribute to his fallen buddies in their own way. By the time of writing, Marco had done more than 1 600 jumps from all kinds of fixed-wing aircraft and helicopters.

The ways 61 Mech veterans find to support each other are simply astonishing at times. Hospital bills are one way – and then there's the very special tribute to Kelvin Luke, the man who saved Marco's life at Smokeshell.

In order to pay for his son's studies, Kelvin sold his beloved motorbike. So his mates from the veterans' motorcycle group, 61 Riders, pooled their resources to get him a new ride. They bought a motorcycle at auction, stripped it down and restored and serviced it. It was better than new when they were done.

When Kelvin arrived at the annual Gariep Dam veterans' weekend, he noticed a mean-looking bike with a matt-black spray job and the 61 flash on the fuel tank. His mates kept a straight face as he kept walking over for another look.

That evening, there was a fireside auction to raise money for veterans in need. Among the memorabilia and other items under the hammer was the bike. The bidding was furious. But when it reached R97 000 they decided it was time to put Kelvin out of his misery. To his astonishment he heard it was all a hoax – the bike was his.

Kelvin was not the only one with misty eyes after that. And soon he was back on the road in the colours of the 61 Riders, for this is Kelvin's way of leaving the past behind him.

There is one more astonishing example of how big-hearted this veteran community is. Andrew Whitaker tells the story:

'The night before the memorial service at the old Smokeshell site, Phia was cleaning the fist-sized wound in HP's back as always. Nicky asked if she could see it and was really shocked. Afterwards, she talked to me about the possibility of crowdfunding to get HP the best possible medical care.'

Andrew discussed it with the 61 veterans' exco, who approved the fundraising bid. Within just a few days, the BackaBuddy fund had amassed more than R400 000, including R150 000 raised by the veterans' Munga cycling team.

These funds were used to book HP into the Wits Donald Gordon Medical Centre in Johannesburg, where he was examined by a highly respected team of surgeons and medical experts. Their feedback was brutally honest: they were prepared to operate on him but warned that he would be under the knife for 12 hours and success was not guaranteed.

When I visited HP and Phia in hospital after he received that feedback, they were not keen on the risk. With more than a hundred operations behind him, HP knew just how long and difficult the recovery from a 12-hour procedure would be for his body and mind. And they've suffered too many disappointments in the past to absorb yet another one.

When I phoned HP as I was typing this, he said all was well but that he was in constant agony. I could hear it in his voice.

PARTING SHOTS

You sit down to write a whole book and when you're done, you're lost for words to thank people properly.

I'm deeply grateful to my 61 brothers who've shown me unconditional friendship simply because we wore the same flash on our uniform sleeves when we were young. The veteran community, in my limited experience, is not about glorifying a war of yesteryear; it is about camaraderie, mutual respect and social support in the here and now. I salute you all.

Thank you to my wife, Yvonne, and son, Sebastian, for their encouragement, putting up with my moods, and endless mugs of tea. To Annie Olivier and her team at Jonathan Ball Publishers, boundless respect for your professionalism and nerves of steel. Last but not least, many thanks to Alfred LeMaitre. This book is all the better for his editing skills and input.

And so ends my unplanned trilogy of veteran journeys. In war movies, the actors talking into military radio handsets always say, 'Over and out!' But that's Hollywood for you.

So from me, as the army taught me correctly 42 years ago: 'OUT!'

Just that.

ABOUT THE AUTHOR

Deon Lamprecht is an author, award-winning journalist and a veteran of 61 Mechanised Battalion Group. He is the author of two books on the Border War, *Tannie Pompie se Oorlog* (2015) and *Die Brug* (2020). This is the first time his work has been translated into English.